Twilight Hours

TWILIGHT HOURS

TWILIGHT HOURS

A Legacy of Verse

By SARAH WILLIAMS

(*SADIE*)

WITH A MEMOIR BY E. H. PLUMPTRE, M.A.

STRAHAN & CO., PUBLISHERS

56, LUDGATE HILL, LONDON

1868

PRINTED BY W. CLOWES AND SONS, DUKE STREET, STAMFORD STREET,
AND CHARING CROSS.

TO

𝔎. and 𝔍. 𝔚.

MOTHER ON EARTH AND FATHER IN HEAVEN

THESE

WITH LOVING THANKS FOR ALL THINGS.

———◆◇◆———

.

'Like as the waves make towards the pebbled shore,
So do our minutes hasten to their end;
Each changing place with that which goes before,
In sequent toil all forwards do contend.'

MEMOIR.

IT is now nearly two years since a small volume
came to me by post, directed to Queen's College,
Harley Street,—

"With the grateful regards of the author, an old
pupil, these first essays in composition."

The book consisted of stories for young children,
and bore the title of "Rainbows in Spring-tide." The
writer hid herself under the *nom de plume* of "Sadie."
I turned over the pages, and found in the tales them-
selves a pleasant ease and genial insight into child-
nature, enlivened here and there with touches of quaint
humour and vivid description. One would have
augured from them that the writer might probably
attain a fair measure of success in the not inglorious
region of the literature of the nursery. But mingling
with the prose there were also, scattered here and there,
brought in with a visible want of connexion which
showed that they belonged to a different mood, and
were the offspring of different hours, a few 'pieces' in
verse. And these, as I read them, seemed to indicate

the possession, if not of high or wide culture, yet of a genius that was real and living. Less than most poetry by young writers did it present the echoes of the greater poets of our time. It had neither the excellences nor the defects of imitative verse. What struck one was its naturalness, its spontaneity, its being the utterance of one who sang "as the birds do," because the song was in her. I quote two samples as showing what led me to wish to know more of the writer :—

"THE SONG OF THE CITY SPARROWS.

"When the summer-time is ended,
    And the winter days are near;
When the bloom hath all departed
    With the childhood of the year ;

"When the martins and the swallows
    Flutter, cowardly, away ;
Then the people can remember
    That the sparrows always stay ;

"That, although we're plain and songless,
    And poor city birds are we,
Yet, before the days of darkness
    We, the sparrows, never flee ;

"But we hover round the window,
    And we peck against the pane,
While we twitteringly tell them
    That the spring will come again.

"And when drizzly dull November
  Falls so gloomily o'er all,
And the misty fog enshrouds them
  In a dim and dreary pall;

"When the streets all fade to dreamland,
  And the people follow fast,
And it seems as though the sunshine
  Was for evermore gone past,—

"Then we glide among the housetops,
  And we track the murky waste,
And we go about our business
  With a cheerful earnest haste;

"Not as though our food were plenty,
  Or no dangers we might meet;
But as though the work of living
  Was a healthy work, and sweet.

"When the gentle snow descendeth,
  Like a white and glistening shroud,
For the year whose life hath ended,
  Floated upward like a cloud;

"Then, although the open country
  Shineth very bright and fair,
And the town is overclouded,
  Yet we still continue there;

"Even till the spring returneth,
  Bringing with it brighter birds,
Unto whom the city people
  Give their love and gentle words;

" And we, yet again descending
   To become the least of all,
Take our name as ' only sparrows!'
   And are slighted till we fall ;

" Still we're happy, happy, happy,
   Never minding what we be ;
For we have a work and do it,
   Therefore very blithe are we.

" We enliven sombre winter,
   And we're loved while it doth last,
And we're not the only creatures
   Who must live upon the past.

" With a chirrup, chirrup, chirrup,
   We let all the slights go by,
And we do not find they hurt us
   Or becloud the summer sky.

" We are happy, happy, happy,
   Never minding what we be ;
For we know the good Creator
   Even cares for such as we."

"THE DAUPHIN IN THE TEMPLE PRISON.

"TO MARIE ANTOINETTE.

" ' O thou, my mother ! dead so long ago,
Who never to my childish joy or woe
Didst say, " That's trifling ;" mother, hear me now ;
Allay the throbbing of my burning brow,
And help me in the problem of my life,
That I may conquer in this vital strife—

A passive strife, to learn no evil thing,
An active strife, to hear no songs they sing !
They beat me for my fingers in my ears,
They beat me for my shock'd, indignant tears ;
O mother, keep me till I come to thee,
Until I from this darkened world shall flee :
So darken'd, for so long a time it seems,
That I can scarcely picture in my dreams
The life we led, before the shadows fell
Which blotted out the face we loved so well !
That face and thine seem never now apart.

   " ' Sweet sister mine, I know not where thou art ;
I sit alone, and through the weary hours
Remember how the years were mark'd with flowers.
It comes across me sometimes with a sting
That I, the captive Louis, am the king.
Poor king ! poor Louis ! poorest orphan ! reft
Of all life's joys at once, and lonely left !
But 'twill not be for long—a streak of light
Which falls celestially serene and bright,
Upon the darkness of my prison floor,
Comes like a promise that 'twill soon be o'er ;
A passing breeze, like thy sweet breath, comes in,
Refines this leaden atmosphere of sin,
And bears my soul upon its wings to thee !
O mother mine, at last thy son is free !'

   " The lips kept mute so long for her dear sake*
Unclosed at length ; it was her name they spake :
Then, closed in sculptured beauty, were at rest ;
The captive king was crown'd among the blest."

---

* " From the time he was told that some admissions of his had been used to condemn his mother to death, the child never spoke until shortly before he died, eighteen months after, in the eleventh year of his age."

As it was, I wrote a note to "Sadie," addressed it
to Messrs. Routledge and Co., the publishers of the
little book, and within a few days there came an
answer, telling me who she was.   Some sixteen
years ago she, as Sarah Williams, had been a pupil
at the College (I lighted on the name by a strange
chance in a faint, half-obliterated pencil class-list,
within a week of this renewed acquaintance) : she had
left it in consequence of illness, had gone on reading
and thinking for herself in a desultory kind of way,
coming very little in contact with what is called
"society," under the influence, as far as her inner
life was concerned, of "pious stragglers from the
Church," but not imbued in any degree with the an-
tagonism of Nonconformity, nor even with its charac-
teristic theology.

There had been nothing eventful in her life so far.
The birth of "Rainbows in Springtide" had been the
first interruption to the calm tenor of a London home,
broken only by visits to Wales or Ramsgate, or the
rarer treat of Paris.   There was as little in the way
of incident in the period—all too short—that followed.
An introduction to Mr. Strahan gained for her admis-
sion to the magazines which issued from his house,
—"Good Words," the "Sunday Magazine," and the
"Argosy,"—and the career of an authoress, more or less

successful, seemed to be opening before her. She had the pleasure of finding herself appreciated. What came to her in payment for her contributions—received with a deprecating wonder that was not without a touch of humour—was to her as a *deodand*, to be disposed of in many acts of kindness to the sick and poor.

And it was clear, the more closely we were brought into contact with her, that hers was one of those characters which success does not spoil—that the power of uttering herself freely tended to ripen both the thoughts that struggled for utterance and the gift of clothing them in words. It was clear, also, that below a nature bright, cheerful, happy—flashing out sometimes into scintillations of genial and fantastic originality, not unlike Elia's—there was a soul working its way through the problems of life as they present themselves to all thinkers, bearing bravely also some special burden of its own. The social sketches which she wrote for the "Argosy," under another *nom de plume*, as "The Foozy Papers," though obviously defective from their limited range of observation, pointed to the possibility of her taking a fair place some day among our lady novelists. The poems which appeared in the other serials I have named, gave promise, as it seemed to me, of something higher. So far as I was able to exercise any influence over her, it was to determine her work in that direction.

So the months passed on. Her father's death, after a few days' illness in January of the present year, gave a great shock to a constitution which had never been strong. For some weeks her visits to us became infrequent. On leaving town for the Easter holidays of the present year, I received from her a small memorial gift, with a few words of what seemed only a kind greeting for the season. When I returned, it was to learn that those few words were to be the last; that the gift had been sent with the consciousness that it might be in very deed in memory of one who had passed away. She had had to make the choice, so often forced upon sufferers, between the certainty of long lingering agony and the possibility of deliverance from it, accompanied by the risk of a more immediate close. Acting on the counsel of friends and medical advisers, she embraced the latter alternative, with apparently a foreboding clear to herself, though not disclosed to others, of what the end would be. And so that end came; and she slept and was at rest. With this presentiment, as of one who saw the shadows deepening round her, not without sadness, but altogether without fear or murmur, and with a heart that thought even then of others rather than herself, she

wrote a "farewell," which after her death, was given
to the friends for whom she had most regard.   It may
fitly find its place here :—

> " City of many sorrows, fare thee well ;
>   Clasped in thy dusky arms, dear comrades dwell.
>   Comfort them, Mother, keep thou them this night ;
>   Breathe on them softly, let their cares lie light,
>   And if they feel me watching through their sleep,
>   Let them not see mine eyes as those that weep ;
>   Let me not bring to them one thought of pain,
>   But calmly pass, like some far distant strain
>   Of rugged music, borne on summer wind,
>   God's air between us—discords all refined
>   To subtlest harmonies, while halting speech,
>   Grown inarticulate, doth deeper reach.
>   Tell them, O Mother City, monitress,
>   That not defect of love, but love's excess,
>   Doth hold me quiet now, doth still my heart,
>   And teach me that true lovers never part."

It is obvious that these are very scanty materials for
a biography.   Nor is the absence of events compen-
sated, in any full measure, by a large mass of corre-
spondence.   Living in a comparatively narrow home-
circle, not recognised by her friends as one who was
likely to win her way to fame, and whose letters were
on that account worth keeping, comparatively few
seem to have been kept.   The greater part of the
correspondence placed in my hands had its starting-
point in her business relations with the two publishing

houses with which her work as an authoress brought
her into contact, and were addressed to Mr. Strahan,
and to the literary adviser of Messrs. Routledge and
Sons. She appears to have welcomed the open-
ing thus given, and uttered herself more freely to
them because there were not in their case the
restraints of previous acquaintance.   They, at all
events, recognised, both of them, that they had a
correspondent who was an exception to the common
run of letter-writers, in almost every one of whose
notes there were some exceptional touches of humour,
or pathos, or imagination.

Extracts from the letters thus kept may help the
readers to understand the character which speaks to
them through the poems in this volume.   They will
acknowledge, if I mistake not, that they are worth
keeping for their own sake.   Those who knew her
will remember with what a sudden gleam of wit, or
abrupt opening of inner depths of thought, her con-
versation was by turns solemnised and illumined.   I
quote from a short memorial paper in " Good Words "
for the present year a thoughtful analysis of the im-
pressions thus left on the minds of those who were
brought more or less closely into contact with her :—

" She was so bright, so light, so airy in her moods and manners,
and yet there was in all a strange undernote, a pathetic chord,

that only made itself heard after the verse had ceased, filling the silence like a speech. There was such light banter in her mirth, such tricksy innocent flashes of fun, mingled with such possibilities of sadness, tears, despair. And ever breaking through the light dancing music she so delighted in, there was a sense of trouble and repressed sorrow, often communicating a kind of unpolished hurry to her finest work. At first one felt a little surprised at this, for the presence of power was unmistakable ; soon one came to expect it; it symbolized that process of painful pressure and determined bracing of the will in the midst of incessant pain by which she came at her best work. Deepest glimpses, touches almost perfect in truth and delicacy, and melodious turns, inimitable in their individuality and freedom, always followed a point or line that was specially disappointing. It was as though her signal for the feast was a sudden and wayward trumpet blare. And it was very much the same with her conversation ; brilliant, sparkling, vivacious as it was in the main, she would throw out un -expectedly the most trying 'posers,' weighty with meaning and purpose. When all were fairly nonplussed over the untoward puzzle, she would cast upon it such rippling lights of humour that it dissolved in genial currents of laughter. She had the faculty of the true humorist—could laugh most lightly when she felt most seriously, and veil her gravest lessons under the kindly mask of mirth.

> " ' Ever across the caustic of her words
>   There dropped the wondrous nectar of her smile,
>   A smile as joyous, frank, and innocent,
>   As that with which a babe awakes from sleep.'

*   *   *   *   *

"Notwithstanding her remarkable quickness and readiness of intellect, there was something strangely far withdrawn and absent about her. When she listened to you, very often it seemed as

b

though she had to summon her soul from far to do rightful service
to the ear; and her answers were so invariably coloured by this
circumstance that not seldom they appeared to the listener start-
ling and enigmatic.   But all who knew her can understand this
now, and understand too, how in her poems, the discipline of
pain and the pleasantness of death hold such a place.   The in-
visible hand stretched forth from the darkness, say rather from the
excess of light, was near her, and she wrote always under the con-
sciousness of this.   She bravely hid her sufferings that the inno-
cent enjoyment of others might be unshadowed by her pain; and
though she treated little trials lightly, no one could have been
warmer, more considerate, or have shown more womanly wile in
her ways of giving sympathy when sympathy was really needed.
She might have used in reference to herself the words she put
into the mouth of another—

" 'Human by birthright of pain, and free of the guild of woe;
   Tender by thorns in the heart, so that our kindred may trust
     me;
   Dropping not gall, but balm, as you did, where'er I go.' "

What follows calls for little comment.   It will be
better to let it tell its own tale.

She vindicates her adherence to her *nom de plume:*—

" I am willing to appear quite anonymously, and I would yield
altogether to your reasoning were 'Sadie' only a *nom de plume;*
but the name, self-given they say in baby-days, has so grown
with me, has become so literally a part of me, that I could lose
both the others with less sacrifice of identity.   In fact, I am
Sadie or nobody, which it shall be I leave to you."

　　　*　　　*　　　*　　　*　　　*

" Thanks for the query about my own name.   It is more com-
fortable to know how to address people; but I suppose most of

us have two or three titles and characters to match. At home
and with my friends I have always been Sadie, so self-named,
they say, before I could speak plain. Sarah is my grim, business
signature, which at first used to make me feel as if I had been
starched. Miss Williams belongs to me, as never having had a
sister, nor, for that matter, a brother."

She looks out on sea and sky, and notes how they
have impressed her. The poet's mind can find sus-
tenance even on the sands of Ramsgate :—

"The weather is celestial, a lazy sea, a smiling sky, with little
wisps of white mist floating about like the ghosts of pleasant
dreams."

    *   *   *   *   *

"Yesterday I saw the sunset over the fields ; there was such a
curious bright peacefulness over everything, the cool clear grey
and blue of the sky, joined to the low green hills by a crimson
line, where the sun had flung back a parting *resurgam* before he
sank."

    *   *   *   *   *

"In this delicious weather one must keep out all day ; this
afternoon the sunset colours on the sea were exquisite, and the
sky scenery magnificent—little gem-like bits of darkest blue set
in snowy curled *cumuli* and lead-grey *nimbus*. Of course it is
utterly impossible to describe this sort of thing ; but I suppose
one's instinct of speech is ineradicable. Talking of instincts, I
fancy the desire for some kind of audience or public is one almost
universal. The few children there are on the sands now, play
among themselves prosaically enough ; but a grown-up person
has only to sit down amongst them, looking tolerably good-
tempered, and may at once enliven them into attempting wonderful
feats, casting up droll little glances in search of a smile of appro-

b 2

bation or amusement. I think, with children at least, that it is partly the unselfish desire to give pleasure. They like gathering shells or doing anything for anybody. I hear dismal accounts of east winds in London; but the swallows believe in the spring, at any rate. They keep arriving in long V-like lines. How tame they are when they first come! One alighted nearly at my feet this morning and stood looking at me with the most charming air of disdain imaginable. Then he perched on a lump of chalk, and gave his greeting to the land in a little low song—only two or three notes—but wonderfully clear and sweet. The gaunt old cliff seems to have a fluttering veil of melody thrown over it, it is so peopled with divers birds."

She records the impression left on her by the books with which her new or old friends supplied her :—

"I have read some capital papers of Lewes' in the 'Fortnightly Review' on the 'Principles of success in Literature,'—rather heathenish,—I think he has a tendency that way ; but solid, original, and thoughtful. Oddly enough, the paper on 'Style' concluded with, I believe, two (of course unintentional) examples of tautology. I suppose it is something like those grammatical errors which were always found in the prefaces of grammars, till they left off having prefaces. What a never-failing comfort any kind of art is."

* * * * *

"I had a sabbath feast yesterday in the 'Unspoken Sermons.' It is not much to say that they are above any spoken ones that I ever heard. My experience of sermons has been unhappy ; but some of the passages are simply the finest utterances of the soul that I ever came across—as 'a condition which, if delusive, would indicate a devil, may, of growth, indicate a saint,'—and so the whole of the 'Higher Faith.'"

* * * * *

"I don't know how the good people do who are always lowly-minded; for me, when I am humble, I am detestable, fit only to growl in a hole like an Adullamite bear. I was just longing for some moral caustic to apply to set me right, when, after the bountiful fashion of Heaven, came instead the sweet and whole-some manna of encouragement."

*   *   *   *   *

"I cannot criticise this work. It is a great pity that it is so unfinished. A pity that is, for art's sake; the public would simply gape at it. So far as regards the author, I don't know, but it is work over which a soul is likely to reel or to harden —only Milton's blindness saved him from either or both, if indeed he was saved. Alas! deep down in my heart lies the doubt whether any such work is right, whether it may not come under the anathema at the end of the Revelation, on those who 'add to the words of the Book.' I think the writer would be held innocent, the work condemned, as God so often seems to take our sins out of us against our will. This I give most doubt-fully; I may transgress it myself to-morrow. There is an in-dividual law for every artist—to his own Master he standeth or falleth. If any of the Bible outlines call for filling in, it is certainly that of the Betrayer. The magnanimity of the Master seems to have held back the abhorrence of his disciples, or that abhorrence is so deep that we get no view of the traitor that would in a story justify—in the sense of *lead to*—his deed. In a fiction, speaking reverently, Judas would be daringly improbable by the rudest canons. This writer has made of him a character dramatically true as Milton's Satan is dramatically true; but both are, in my conviction, morally false."

*   *   *   *   *

"I am afraid the author of ———— would not approve of my criticisms. Novices are always Draconian, you know, and my first impulse would be to pitch the whole thing into the fire; my second to write to the author and tell him that I was very sorry, and that he was an ill-used genius. I can fancy that books of that order are both more irritating and more common than real trash. It seems to be so in everything. An absolutely worthless man would almost be interesting as a curiosity. The street-boy problem consists not in the actual but the possible thief, and among our acquaintances those who are thoroughly stupid or ill-natured are no trouble—we simply drop them and forget them. Those who fret us are the people that ought to be charming,—would be, but for some defect or deforming excrescence that we dare not even try to pluck out, lest the whole moral nature bleed to death."

*   *   *   *   *

"Thank you so much for letting me see Mr. Macdonald's poems ; some parts one can read over and over like Bible words, with that mingling of sympathy and reverence that is one of the joys of life ; but I think his poetic feeling masters him, instead of his mastering it—a possible beauty in the man, but a flaw in the artist. * * * * Mr. Swinburne fails, if he does fail, from the opposite excess. I can fancy him really enjoying himself over his poetry, like a reckless rider on a good horse. Only Shakespeare—'Il Divino'—combines the two types—trills out 'Who is Sylvia?' and sighs, with deep content, 'There's a Divinity doth shape our ends.'"

*   *   *   *   *

"Mr. Macdonald says, in this month's 'Guild Court,' 'only God can satisfy a woman.' Surely God can satisfy a poet ?"

*   *   *   *   *

"I have been reading Miss Greenwell's poems, and like some of them very much. * * * They are not musical, but they are poetical : and since it seems that we must give up one, the music must go, as soul is higher than sense. Nevertheless for

me, personally, a poem is a thing that sings.   One suffers from
the dim weight of one's own soul, never from sense.   I see some
of them have been set to music, but that proves nothing.   Musical
words seldom set well: they have the tune in them already, and
will not take another."

*   *   *   *   *

"As to Swinburne, I believe he has so much power over me
that he will not let me read his bad things ; in the Poems and
Ballads, the pages turned over as though some one else was turning
them, till at the wonderful Litany the invisible presence said
'Halt!' I began and ended with that.   One such poem is
enough, not for a morning's reading, but for a lifetime, if only
the last two lines might be prophetic—

> ' The gold is turned to a token,
>   The staff to a rod,
> Yet thou shalt bind up them that are broken,
>   O Lord our God !'"

'   *   *   *   *   *

"I find no reason why I should not read Swinburne's Poems:
certainly I had little more than an hour, and so perhaps had only
time to get the good in them.   And of course it is possible that I
may have read something very bad without knowing it: in which
case it cannot have done me much harm.   It is really comical,
after entering a book, as one would a fish-market, ready to close
eyes and nose, to find one's self in a grand heathen oratorio :—
heathen certainly, but, all the more for that, with a deep pathetic
truth underlying its despair and unrest.   Surely such music cannot
be destined for Satan's palaces.   *   *   *   Do you remember
how Sir Walter Scott resolved to give up writing poetry after
reading Byron ?   One could scarcely help coming to the same
determination after Swinburne; only, I suppose, it would be like

resolving not to talk,—more laudable than possible. Would it be too brave to weave these into the improvising?

"TO A. C. SWINBURNE.

"I dare not rhyme within the poet's court,
  Nor shake my jingling bells against his harp;
  But if my greeting can but solace him,
  If all unconsciously he hear my voice
  Cry 'Elder brother, hail! God comfort thee,
  And give to thee a golden harp one day;'
  If he can feel a friend's hand in the dark,
  Then I am glad : if not, I am content
  To reverence in silence."

Here are a few touches of her love of children, and her conscious appreciation of their unconscious humour :—

"Her song to 'Heartsease' (she is speaking of a dear friend), is dedicated to me, and my little book 'Rainbows in Spring' is dedicated to her nephew, Bertie, such a loveable child, especially when he is naughty. The other day, for some misdemeanour, he was dismissed from the dinner-table by his mamma. Bertie finding himself landed with his little plate in the bedroom, not unnaturally objected, remonstrating through the keyhole—'I can't eat my dinner in here—a bedroom isn't the proper place to eat dinners in ; I won't have my dinner here.' 'Then you will go without,' said the mother. 'Very well,' said Bertie, resignedly, 'then I shan't have my dinner, and then I shall be ill, and then I shall die; and when I am dead I will fetch a policeman, and you shall be hanged.' A tolerable notion of climacteric oratory for a child of four years old. But Bertie has his tender moods when he comes to his aunt, saying, ' Auntie Bessie, kiss me, as though you loved me.' "

* * * * *

"For three weeks I was alone—it was queer but pleasant. There is a curious rest in perfect solitude. Long ago when I was a little child, I remember sobbing out that 'I should always be good if there were no people in the world,'—nice sentiment, as I was always begging for some little girl to tea."

* * * * *

" Bertie's sister Daisy said rather a good thing the other day. She was troublesome, and her mamma said, ' Daisy, if you bother me so, I shall give you to the butcher, and then what will you do ?' ' Then I shall bother the butcher,' said Daisy, tranquilly ; tolerably cool and clear for two years old—at least she is not three yet !' "

* * * * *

" We had a visitation yesterday from a cousin, aged eleven, who talks of demanding a latch key, because it is ' such a nuisance,' he says, ' to be fetched home directly after supper.' He is rather a young Philistine."

* * * * *

"Bertie gave me his views of his future career, to the effect that if cabmen have a monument in St. Paul's he will be a cabman ; if not, a general."

* * * * *

" I am afraid you will not be so romantic as our old postman, who, when somebody once sent me a Rimmel's Almanack, begged for the almanack to lay among his things, to give him pleasant fancies. Poor fellow ! he died of the gout not long after."

* * * * *

"One of my child-friends is getting jealous of Bertie, whom she knows only by name. She said the other day, 'It is all in a muddle: Johnny Rowe loves me, but I love you, but you love Bertie, and I dare say he loves somebody else.' Not at all improbable, nor a bad *résumé* of things in general—say in a novel."

Other extracts must be taken as they come *de omnibus rebus*, each lit up by some gleam of light fancy or solemnised by the undertone of some deep thought :—

"April 13, 1867.

"Special thanks for the little poem of 'A Life.' Some lives would seem to be scarcely complete without death ; it comes as such a beautiful, harmonious rounding off ; with others of us it is a horrible discord, the sudden snap of a tiger's tooth ; the letter made me cry, it seemed such a pity for the friendship to be broken ; only, God knows best. I have not had many sorrows in my life ; but, looking back even already, I would not be without one of them."

*   *   *   *   *

"Apropos to nothing, Why is it that the Scotch say, 'Puir body,' and the English, 'Poor soul?' Do the Scotch think the soul never needs pity ; or do they turn it over to their ministers, as they would their clothes to a tailor ?"

*   *   *   *   *

"Somebody asked me once what I should do if I found myself at the head of a household ? I said 'Abdicate,' with the promptitude of instinct ; but even that is not possible with such dreadfully conscientious people, who will not impose upon one comfortably."

*   *   *   *   *

"I keep all her scoldings. She taught me singing once, and has taught me *living* ever since. You would like her. She is an embodied repose—half a lifetime wiser than I, but only six years older."

* * * * *

"Is it not a shame for Gladstone * to have been used so, set up as a brilliant mark for the daws to peck at? Let them peck! they are but daws after all; and the eagle wounded, is an eagle still. Only, this our England has not progressed so rapidly of late years, that we can contentedly see her drawn back because the leader is too much of a Pegasus. Well, happily, I have no business with politics. There is a certain sense of snugness in absolute insignificance. Also, it is going to rain, and I am always good when it rains. There is such a curious lullaby in the sweet pure rush of water, cleansing away foulnesses and dust, like a heavenly air blowing through our error and strife."

* * * * *

"The grain of the Deity that is within us makes it impossible for us to conceive a nature beyond man as other than a nobler man. We instinctively give the Almighty a worthy foe, but I think we are wrong. I believe Satan is the meanest spirit in creation; that it is a significant truth which places hell down in the depths—that 'without are dogs.'"

* * * * *

"It is a flaw—I am afraid a fatal flaw in me—that I cannot do any good by taking pains, any more than a tree can try to grow: only the Great Master is a perfect gardener. If He means to make me a 'goodly plant' He will do it; if not, the place I long for some one else will fill. There are no empty niches in creation, and there is room for unfinished souls in heaven."

* * * * *

---

* Written after the Oxford Election of 1865.

" This is certainly the millennium of the Smiths."

      *   *   *   *

" I was at the Academy on Tuesday (in 1866) for five hours. There is one little painting of a bough of apple-blossom that would alone be worth going for. The exquisite freshness of the picture seems absolutely to pervade the room ; but the gem of the whole collection, I think, is Noel Paton's 'Mors Janua Vitæ,' for thought, and poetry, and power.

" The story is told in an extract from 'The good Fight,' but this is scarcely needed ; every detail is so eloquent. The Christian knight, led by an unseen presence along his dark and untortuous way, his triumph laid aside in the jewelled sword which he leaves behind ; his dead hopes lying beneath his feet as withered leaves ; his armour bright, only because it will not take a stain ; so through conflict, and darkness, and pain, he presses on, till the supreme moment comes. Then the shadowy angel lays her hand on his shoulder with the touch of death, and with the agony comes the ecstacy ; the veil is drawn back, a glory of light shines in from heaven. The shadow is seen to be an angel ; Death is swallowed up in Life. This is the moment of the picture ; a climax so extreme that the slightest failure anywhere would be terribly disappointing, but there is none.

" The face and figure of the knight seem perfect, and the angel is the only angel I ever saw who was neither a pale nega- tion nor a sensuous woman. The way in which the artist contrives to give the joyful brightness of her colouring, and yet keep her perfectly spiritual, is something wonderful."

      *   *   *   *   *

" What a dreadful piece of bosh that is ' an honest man's the noblest work of God ! ' To say nothing of the angels—a good woman is infinitely higher—not than a good man though ; so there we come back again."

      *   *   *   *   *

"One of the compensations belonging to an impatient nature is, that it soon burns itself out into the grey ash of indifference; also, it was an early habit of mine to wipe my sums off the slate directly they were finished."

*　　*　　*　　*　　*

"This is a curiously independent little district, everyone follows his own sweet will, and things happen according to a fortuitous *concourse* of atoms. The police are so unpopular that the maids have all taken to smile on the postmen, and the result is, not to facilitate the delivery of letters. I saw one beaming youth emerge from an area some fifteen minutes late, his bag thrown contemptuously across his shoulder, and his radiant gaze bent upon a photograph; of course, under such circumstances, I yielded in contented acquiescence on receiving a letter addressed J. Woodhouse, Esq., while my own poor letter wandered off into space."

*　　*　　*　　*　　*

"A dictum of Goethe's has burnt into my convictions, namely, that to believe in anything one must live in solitude."

*　　*　　*　　*　　*

"There is a dreamy meditative organ meandering in the distance, one of those tunes that, as Mrs. Poyser says, keep on asking questions, and insist on one's attempting to answer such puzzles as *Cui bono*—anything? *Quien sabe*—anything? As I heard a clever man say he had once, for three months, doubted his own existence; but it was in his youth, before he had rheumatism."

*　　*　　*　　*　　*

"Don't you like political women? I do—they scold so."

*　　*　　*　　*　　*

"I am so sorry; such a panorama of people have been marching through this week of mine, that I totally forgot."

*　　*　　*　　*　　*

"I think you wrote in a self-depreciative mood.   One gets them sometimes, at least I do, berating myself, and scarifying my mental epidermis till it is quite tender.   But, *entre nous*, I never find myself any better for the process.   I believe that the law of tonics is reversed in morals, and it is not the bitter things that invigorate.   This morning I sat out on the rocks watching the tide come in ; it was wonderfully pleasant.   The mighty river in the distance, and the gentle tender little ripple close by, while the waves were shaded purple and green, and the distant clouds looked, as distant clouds somehow always do look, *home-like.*"

*   *   *   *   *

"Your letter arrived opportunely in the midst of our first winter fog—one of those black mornings when, by the help of letters and a fire, one can hug oneself in cat-like content ; but without such accessories would find the world 'flat, stale, and unprofitable.'"

*   *   *   *   *

"Well, it is nice to have been young, but I like being old best ; one does not fit into the world at first somehow, and tender flesh will wince at getting its corners rubbed off."

*   *   *   *   *

"If he objects to the thing itself as not natural, I hope to get and to deserve that censure much more by-and-by : it is one of my few deep convictions that the supernatural is natural, that in the moral world, as in the physical, lightnings, volcanoes, ava-lanches, are as truly natural as fish-ponds and croquet-grounds. Nature includes all.   Art should include all, only let each artist take the department that suits him.   The *supernatural* needs a man's strength and depth ; the *exceptionally natural* is the ground I mean to take and work, God helping me.   Now you have my confession of faith artistic.   Only you and I well know the chasm between the endeavour and the result.   It would be ludicrous, if it were not pathetic, to compare purpose and production."

* * * * *

"Home worries" (speaking of her mother's illness) "always seem to me the worst troubles ; those out-of-doors are lighter just because they are out-of-doors, and they are generally susceptible of cool business-like consolation. In personal sorrow we can 'commune with our own hearts and be still,' and, under the night veil of silence, bury our dead out of our sight ; but home cares come just between the two—it is neither the *sanctum sanctorum*, nor the outer court of the temple—and so the sellers of doves and the money-changers get in and play havoc with our peace."

* * * * *

"If it was only possible, I have the best intentions in the world to devise something super-excellent ; but when a poor body's brains turn clayey it is of no use digging for flints therein."

* * * * *

"Last Saturday I was too much shrivelled up by the cold to speak the thanks I felt. Some states of the atmosphere benumb me altogether, as though a dumb spirit walked the air and clutched away all power of speech."

The natural reticence of a nature like hers in dealing with the depths of her own life, led her, in writing to those who were comparatively strangers, to say but little that would find a place in what are called distinctively "religious" biographies. But that little is at once real and precious, and I cannot better close the series which I have put together than by two or three short utterances which show what the writer of these poems was in her acts and her prayers for others.

The first is in acknowledgment of a payment for literary work, which seemed to her in excess of what she had a just claim to :—

"The other half would in any case be God's money. Could you not use that for some good deed ?"

What follows was written for the friend in whose love she found one of the great blessings of her life :—

"A joyous new year! May God our Father bless you and keep you and hold you close to Himself; then you will be safe and happy. * * *

"Adieu, my darling. God bless you: Christ keep you: the Holy Ghost be near you."

I know not if I have succeeded in bringing before those who read these pages the living picture which stands out so distinctly in my own memory. I have not thought it right,—scanty as the materials were, occupied, as I am, with other things,—to decline the task. The fact that it was my lot unconsciously to exercise some influence over the growth of "Sadie's" mind, when she was just passing into girlhood, that the later years of her life again brought us into contact, and gave me the opportunity of determining, in some degree, the form of her literary work, seemed a sufficient reason to me why I, in the absence of any better qualified, should undertake this office, leaving to others the task of collecting and editing her 'Remains.' Others must judge how I have fulfilled it. I shall be content if I have not altogether disappointed those who knew her, if I have led some who did not know her to sympathise and love.

There has been, I need not say, a sorrowful pleasantness in reviving these recollections of a life that passed away before it had attained, as we judge, its full ripeness, growing into the " blade " and the " ear," but not " the full corn in the ear." One remembers it now with some touch of regret that more was not done for it and by it on earth, but also with the confident hope that all its capacities will grow elsewhere to their full stature, and all its cravings be satisfied in the light of God's presence, and all its incompleteness become full-orbed in the completeness of the Eternal. To quote her own words once again :— " The Great Master is a perfect gardener. . . . . . . There is room for unfinished souls in Heaven."

E. H. P.

November 23rd, 1868.

c

CONTENTS.

~~~~~~~~

THE DOOM OF THE PRYNNES.

SONGS OF COMRADES.

QUESTIONINGS.

RESPONSES.

SOSPIRI VOLATE.

NATURE APOSTATE.

CHILD POEMS.

LAMENTS.

BROKEN CHORDS.

BAAL.

BAAL.

I.

BAAL, we cry to thee from morning till even,
    With the cry of the beasts that are slain, and of men that
        are wounded;
Wilt thou not hear us, O Baal, the god of our fathers?
By the anguish of life and of death let the gods be entreated:
        Hear us, O Baal.

Deafness and dumbness hath Baal, the god of the
    heathen;
Yet through the cry of the people there pierceth a
    whisper,
Far as the distance of God, yea, far off as the
    heavens,

Near with the nearness of man, heart to heart with
    his brother,
Sweet with the infinite music of infinite loving,
So that the mountains should melt, and the clouds,
    at his coming,
Mournful as one that doth call finding none to regard
    him :—

Behold, I stand at the door and knock, but ye will not
    open;
Ye will not come unto me, and taste of life;
All day I wait with mine outstretched arms, and ye will
    not enter;
I fain would fold you beneath my wings, but ye will not
    come.

II.

𝔅𝔞𝔞𝔩, we cry to thee from morning till even,—
In the noon of the world now we cry to thee, Baal, all mighty;
Not with the slaughter of brutes and the smiting of body,

But with rending of soul and of strength, with a sacrifice
human,
With the blighting of youth, and the fading away of our
manhood:

Hear us, O Baal.

Deafness and dumbness hath Baal, the god of the
heathen;
Still through the ages resoundeth the voice of the Just
One,
Calm with the calmness of woe overcome and accom-
plished:
Having ascended, He sitteth at rest with the Father,
Waiting the fulness of time, His atonement's fruition—
Awful in calmness and strength is the voice of the Just
One:—

The gospel have they, the law and light, but they will
not hearken.
My Spirit shall not for ever strive with man;
Though one should rise from the dead, they would not
observe nor profit;
The tree that falleth to south or north, as it falls must
lie.

III.

Baal, we cry to thee from morning till even,—
In the eve of creation we cry to thee, Baal the Ancient;
Shelter us, shadow of Baal, from Him, the Supernal;
Let the mountains of Baal fall on us, and cover our faces.
Hateful in light is the Day-Spring eternal:
　　　　Hear us, O Baal.

Deafness and dumbness hath Baal, the god of the
　　　heathen;
Only the voice of the Judge rolleth down on the
　　　thunder.
He whom they pierced they shall look on, and know
　　　that they pierced Him;
Fearful in sternness the love cast aside and despisèd,
Sorrow encrystalled to wrath, as the mountains un-
　　　bending;
Even the sun in his strength fades to darkness before
　　　Him :—

Omega,—close ye the book, and seal it, 'tis now the ending;

He that is unjust, let him be unjust still;

Depart, ye cursed and blind, depart into outer darkness;

I know ye not, as ye knew not me in the time gone by.

IV.

Baal, we cry to thee from morning till even,—

In the night that is endless we cry to thee, Baal the Tyrant.

See to it, Baal the False, our allegiance is failing;

In the fire that consumeth, our nature is changing and changing;

Weaker and weaker is waning the evil within us;

And what have we but evil, what have we, when that shall have failed us?

Hear us, O Baal.

Deafness and dumbness hath Baal, the god of the heathen,

But through the silence of ages the Word is approaching;

Back roll the gates on their hinges of darkness, and
    backward
Fall all the vapours of blindness, and falsehood, and
    evil;
He who alone may touch pitch and yet fear no defile-
    ment,
He who was slain and is worthy, the Lamb, the
    Atonement,
Cometh in fulness of time to the spirits in prison :—

Awake, ye dead! I make all things new; let the night
    be ended.
The last one slain is Death, but he shall be slain;
From henceforth there shall be no more curse: whoso
    will, come freely;
The Spirit and Bride say Come, and let him that
    heareth say Come;
For the Star of the morning is risen, the night is over
    and gone.

PASTORALS.

A PASTORAL.

LEIGHTON'S PICTURE—ROYAL ACADEMY, 1867.

THERE, where our fingers meet,
  That is the true note, Sweet :
Lean your head, so, on my breast,
  For the full deep tone ;
Let the white on the brown hand rest,
  Fairest, mine own.

Folded in rose-leaf mouth,
Honey secure from drouth ;
Blessèd are these among reeds,
  By the flower-breath fed :
Jealous Pan from his place of weeds
  Thrusts forth his head.

Flutter not, perfumed air;
Lift not her tresses fair,
Stir not the soul from its sleep;
  Let the tune dream on:
In the time when we wake to weep
  All will be gone.

FINETTE

FINETTE was young, Finette was fair,
    And never a lover had she;
Finette she cried, in her young despair,
    "'T were better we never should be;
The dance will go, and it irks me so,
    Here by the lonely tree."

Gerôme was hale, but Gerôme was pale,
    For a lover he fain would be,
And he would not know, though they told him so,
    That the maiden he chose was free;
So Gerôme he stood in the dusky wood,
    And a sorrowful wight was he.

Finette she said, as she raised her head,
  " Somebody watches for me."
Gerôme he said, with a lofty head.
  " My lady is looking for me."
Gerôme came one, and Finette came two,
  Two little steps half way ;
Gerôme he sighed, and Finette she cried,
  But never a tear had they.
The dance is done, but the game is won,
  Merrily ends the day.

UNDER THE MULBERRY TREE.

I.

DROPPING fruit, and leaves that quiver,
　　Where the sunshine trembles through;
Slumberous sighs the sleeping river,
　　Summer winds the flowerets woo;
　　　Drowsily the humming bee
　　　Murmurs forth his melody.

Black with crimson, luscious berries
　　Hang our tent, like perfumed bells—
Bells to ring-in far-off fairies
　　From the many-coloured dells;
　　　Mossy root for fairy seat,
　　　Mushroom stool for fairy feet.

Sweetest wine for softest pressing,
　　Aromatic, running o'er;
Leaves and lips alike caressing:
　　Plenty still doth rule the store;
　　　Surely all the sun must be
　　　Underneath our feasting tree.

I.

Rain-drops, tear-drops,
All the world is weeping;
Not a sorrow lieth still,
Streaming clouds have drowned the hill,
And the sun is sleeping.

White clouds, bright clouds,
Through the nimbus peeping,—
Is it thunder, is it rain?
Will the darkness come again?
Or the light up-creeping?

Swift light, strong light,
O'er the zenith sweeping;
Now the sun awakes to reign,
Sweetness overcometh pain,
Joy from sorrow reaping.

III.

Softly the twilight is falling, is falling,
   Over the mountain and over the lea ;
Softly the cuckoo is calling, is calling,
    "Oh my love, Oh my love, over the sea !
      Cu-coo, cu-coo."

Slowly the notes, in their infinite longing,
   Drop, as the lily leaves drop on the stream ;
Swiftly the fairies rise, thronging and thronging,
    As the last tones come on daylight's last gleam,
      " Cu-coo, cu-coo."

Silently, silently, homeward together,
   Each with his burden of sweetness and pain ;
Wondering, wondering, under what weather
    Mulberry berries shall bring us again
      To woo, to woo.

HOP-PICKING.

MARY.

OH the heart I used to have,
  Innocent and meek !
Some one stole it suddenly,
  Kissed it from my cheek.
Now the pride of bitterness
  Will not let me speak.

ROBIN.

There she sits, the idle thing,
  Careless as a queen !
Fairer, in good sooth, than all
  Queens that I have seen ;
Queen of all the garden, she
  Knows it well, I ween.

Blossom of the bine is she,
  Gathered in my haste ;
Who would give so fair a thing
  Such a bitter taste ?
Who would think, for such a thing,
  I my life should waste ?

Swaying lightly to and fro,
  Blossom of the bine ;
Any hand may gather it,
  Any hand but mine ;
Any staff will serve for it,
  Such a clinging vine !

MARY.

Some one looks away from me,—
  Let him look away ;
Other men will wait on me,
  Gladly, all the day,
If I had but heart enough
  Always to be gay !

MAR'

OH the heart I
Innocent an
Some one stole it s
Kissed it from m
Now the pride of b
Will not let me s

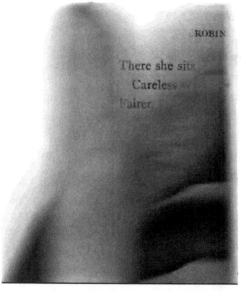

ROBIN

There she sits
Careless
Fairer.

LAYS.

A FACE SEEN AT A WINDOW.

GREY bands of hair that droop towards the grave,
  Still folded lips that shut in history,
Eyes that might come from where the palm-trees wave,
  Shadowed with half unconscious mystery;
Gazing and gazing, till the heavy tears
  Wearily gather, and neglected fall;
Till the pale lips drop off the chain of years,
  Part, with a very child's beseeching call:
" Mother, oh mother!" Then they close again;
Startled, the soul draws back within its pain.

How do the angels bear it, if they hear
  Only the cry that one whole city sends!
Hope writhing in the tyrant grasp of Fear,
  The wail of woe that never turns nor ends.

Only a woman suffering alone,
   Only the rain for common company,
Only my prayer for thee, sister unknown,
   For Christ's dear sake the good God comfort thee!
Meeting a moment, meeting nevermore,
Till we shall smile at all our sorrows o'er.

STREET MUSICIANS.

HARP.

OH the teazing, weary tune,
　　That my fingers will not play !
Oh the worn-out, crazy harp !
　　Shall I fling it quite away ?
No, poor harp, we are old friends,
Comrades, till our journey ends.

CORNET.

If ever a man was a madman,
　　'Twas he who essayed to rise
From a pauper life to an artist life,
　　'Neath the fog of the English skies.
What if the music within him
Should struggle and pant to speak ?

There is never a note to work his will,
And expression is only a thing of skill;
With vision blinded, and utterance weak,
  He may pipe his soul away,
And never a one of the crowd will hear
  The thing that he meant to say.

VIOLIN.

Playing blindly, blindly, blindly,
  I have visions none can see;
Surely Fate hath used me kindly,
  Sights of sadness reach not me.
What though the angel music
  Doth soar above my head?
I meekly follow after,
  With firm and joyful tread.
It is a good, not evil thing,
To know some songs one cannot sing.

There shone a smiling seraph
  Upon the dusty way;
He shook his plumy wings and said
"There comes no failure to the dead,
  Ye rise with me one day."

MINNIE CONNOR.

ALL her tangled hair a-curl,
　　All her tangled thoughts a-whirl,
Lost from off the string, O pearl !
　　　　　　　　Minnie Connor.

Flashing through the crowded streets,
Half a smile for all she meets,
Strangely diverse those she greets.
　　　　　　　　Minnie Connor.

Such bright visions in her eyes,
Such disdainment of disguise,
Such a power to fall or rise.
　　　　　　　　Minnie Connor.

Set in London home to tame,
Like a passion flower a-flame,
In a narrow garden frame.
　　　　　　　　Minnie Connor.

Brother " somewhere,"—laugh it past,—
Father working at his last,
Mother where all work has passed.

Minnie Connor.

Innocent, not ignorant,
She can bitterly descant
On the impotence of cant.

Minnie Connor.

Yet so docile is she still,
Speak her kindly, and she will
Follow you to good or ill.

Minnie Connor.

There's the wrong, that ill is there,
And that, in some brief despair
Which she takes, she will not care.

Minnie Connor.

Wilful, tender, foolish, proud,
One who ne'er in prayer has bowed;
Who will guide her through the crowd?

Minnie Connor.

O FY HÊN GYMRAEG.

"Oh for [a word of] mine own old Welsh!"
The proverbial longing of the Welsh in London.

YES, there is nothing I want, dear,
    You may put the candle by;
There is light enough to die in,
    And the dawning draweth nigh.
Only the want remaineth,
    Gnawing my heart away:
Oh for a word of my mother's tongue,
    And a prayer she used to pray!
        O fy hên Gymraeg!

I wish I had taught you to speak it
    While the light was on my brain;
It has vanished now, with the thousand things
    That will never come back again.

Only a vision of waters
   Rising towards the flow,
Cometh instead of the countless hills,
   The hills that I used to know.
      O fy hên Gymraeg !

The people are frozen hard here—
   Not you, my darling, not you !—
And the air is thick with its yellow fog,
   And the streets have slime for dew.
There is never a line of beauty
   In all the weary rows,
And the saddest thing of the whole is this,
   That the bareness no one knows ;
They are quite contented, and think it fine.
      O fy hên Gymraeg !

Hush thee a moment, dearest,
   A vision is mine just now :
The place where of old we used to play,
   On the edge of the mountain's brow ;

And the time, one sunny morning,
   When a preacher came by that way,
And he talked to us with the gentle words
   That hallowed and blessed our play,
     O fy hên Gymraeg !

We gathered us round about him,
   And we told him our boyish dreams ;
And I saw the light in his deep-set eyes
   Come flashing in tender gleams.
And we said, " Are our visions folly ?
   Should we banish them, and forget ? "
And he answered,—how well I can see him now,
With the shade of the mountain across his brow !—
" There is never a longing the heart can feel,
   But a blessing shall fill it yet."
     Gorphwysfa ! O Gorphwysfa ! *
       Gogoniant ! † Amen.

---

  * *Gorphwysfa :* The name of his home, common in Wales,—
meaning a resting-place.

  † *Gogoniant!* Glory ! The old rallying shout at the open-air
preachings ; said to have first suggested to Handel the idea of
his Hallelujah Chorus.

THE DOOM OF THE PRYNNES.

THE DOOM OF THE PRYNNES.

PART I.

I, BEING then a child, had once two friends,
   My cousins then, my guiding angels since :
We dwelt together in a strange old house,
That, like the fortunes of our family,
Had shrunk and withered to pathetic age ;
Until men said we should some day be crushed,
A nest of eagles 'neath a crumbling rock ;
And yet there was a certain charm in this,
Like living on some cracked volcano side,
That any day might yawn and let us in,
United in the bridal of one death.

   The room we used was once the banquet hall,
With many-coloured windows looking east,
Across a little, quaint, old-fashioned street,
That scarcely suited its locality—
The dark, tumultuous heart of London town.

The walls were oaken, wrought in deep device
Of pomegranates and acorns—once our shield ;
While underneath the mantel one had carved,
With mingled vanity and insolence,
" Here dined with Owain Prynne, King James the
    Small."

  Beneath a northern light my father sat,
Conversing with the stars from night till morn,
While I sometimes would stand beside his knee
And gaze at Cassiopeia, till I saw
" The lady in the chair," and said she had
My cousin Agnes' face, and smiled well pleased,—
She being lady-moon of my young life.
The foolish fancy of a foolish child,
So said my father, while he bade me look
Along the telescope to find out truth.

  Then, through the dark and narrow way I peered,
To see the little star become a sun,
With satellites, and bright mysterious rings,
While finest fragments of the Milky Way
Grew into spheres and systems infinite,
Until I sighed—" God must be very tired,
With such a weight of worlds hung round His neck."

My father frowned rebuke; his brother said,
" The child is still so young, Cadwallader ;
When Agnes was that age I humoured her.
Come hither, Elin, I will show you here
The wonders that lie hidden in the world
Of infusoria."
          So through his glass
I looked, and saw a teeming mass of life,
A seething, writhing, crawling, ashy life,
And cried, " I do not like our world at all,
It is so ghastly ugly underneath."

The savants banished me, and, nothing loth,
I fled to where my cousins were at work—
We all did work, we Prynnes, being sad and poor.
Sweet Agnes wove a silver web of song,
And Mark, her cousin and mine, drove on a pen
That like a thirsty bird drank up the ink.
While I—I taught a most majestic cat
That claws were made for sheathing, not to scratch,
Until the bright-eyed mice came boldly forth,
And puss was useless, being civilized.

I made confession of my latest sins,
And Agnes, while she chode, did comfort me.
" The beauty is there, though we see it not,
'Tis only we are tired, my little heart ;
We see God darkly, through our coloured glass,
As men for safety do observe the sun."
And yet her own life was not all so calm,
For as our dying lamp was not renewed,
She sat with folded hands, and plaintive sang
The hymn of one who, though a Protestant,
Was yet a nun self-clothed in purity :

> " O driving wind, O drifting rain,
>   O force and weakness, joined in pain,
>   Fit parable for me.
>   Just so, I know and will the right,
>   And err, and work my soul's despite,
>   In sin and misery.

> " O little children in the street,
>   With patient, holy, pattering feet,
>   And ever-ready smile ;
>   I pray you, draw my soul to yours,
>   And hold it when it feebly soars,
>   Lest Satan me beguile.

" O misty twilight, grey and wan,
  That like a ghost steals darkly on,
    And halts not, nor relents ;
I dare not front your visage pale,
Nor come within your solemn veil,
    Until my soul repents :

" Repents of woman's need and claims,
  Of instincts, passions, holiest aims,
    And clinging, beating heart ;
Although I would not have it so,
The spirits will not rise and go
    Because I cry, ' Depart.'

" What though I kneel like marble saint,
  My very soul grows sick and faint
    At thought of such repose ;
My hands may clasp in stony calm,
But, each on each, the throbbing palm
    In burning anguish glows.

" Oh, Jesus, son of Mary, hear,
  And in Thy plenitude draw near,
    And piteously forgive :

As Thou didst live all sanctified,
As Thou in solitude hast died,
   Help me to die, and live."

  Agnes had sung, as sings the summer wind
That dies away in shadows; but Mark's voice
Came thunderous, like some Gregorian chant,
With neither harmony nor melody,
But roughened largeness in its monotone :

   "I, standing here, fling back my agony
   Against the brazen glory of the sky ;
   Ye brutish clouds, that all insensate lie,
   And smile, and smile, in blandest idiocy,
   Ye are but low, although ye seem to be
   Above our earth so very calm and high,
   For depth is height, and heart-deep is my cry,
   Man only fathoms human agony."

   I shivered, Agnes drew me to her side.
" The child is shaken with our stormy winds."
" 'The child !' " Mark cried, " 'tis evermore ' the
      child : '
If I were dying, you would moan, ' The child !'
If I were dead, you still would sigh, ' The child !' "

She bent to kiss me, but between our lips
There fell a crystal tear that parted them,
And held them parted, like magician's spell;
And then I knew, as children know such things,
That not my life, nor love, nor deathless soul,
Could weigh, with her, against a hair of his;
Knew it, and loved her utterly the while.

Mark turned and left us: Agnes watched him go,
Like one who sees a sudden, angry sun
Drop down behind the threatening, smoking hills,
To rise upon the ruins of a world.
Yet still she sang to me in notes sad-sweet.

" Sleep, little sister, sleep! the flowers are nodding
    weary;
Over the mountain-tops steal shadows, soft and slow;
Dreaming thy happy dreams, my love shall still be
    near thee,
Into the fairy-land together we will go.

" Sleep, little sister, sleep ! the bees have ceased their
    humming;
Swiftly the forest birds have vanished with the light,

Only the nightingale from out the wood is coming,
  Singing her tender song, as though she wooed the
    night.

" Sleep, little sister, sleep ! the stars, God's eyes, are
    beaming
  Lovingly o'er the world, as night more darkly falls ;
Shadows that hide from Him are only mortal seeming,
  He is awake to hear the feeblest babe that calls.
Sleep, little sister, sleep,
Sleep, sleep !"

  And then, o'er all the trouble of the day,
A downy veil of tranquil stillness stole,
And with her arm beneath my head I dreamt
It was God's heart on which I rested, safe.

Part II.

MARK wrote too much, and hated what he wrote,
   Till Agnes said " I must pen ' leaders ' too."
Whereat he answered, " Here is my receipt,—
Sneer at the Emperor, Cobden, and John Bright ;
Declare that Gladstone is too eloquent,
And that the peril of the land demands
A jocund premier.

                         Prove that working men
Are brutal, fools, with Machiavellian skill ;
That they will climb to power as Satan climbed,
To fall as Satan fell, and— Let me see :
No, that was Samson—drew the gates down with him."
And then, across the caustic of his words,
There dropped the wondrous nectar of his smile,
A smile as joyous, frank, and innocent
As that with which a babe awakes from sleep.

" Why fret your conscience, cousin, writing thus ? "

So Agnes pleaded.   Mark said, " Life is sweet."

" And roses are so dear."   Reproachfully
She glanced to where, for nearly all the year,
A vase of roses stood beside her hand.

" They make life's sweetness.   Agnes sing to me ;
'Tis better than rebuking—juster, too."
She, docile, sang a simple village lay:—

> " Down the mountain came the stream,
>   Leaping in the glowing beam
>   From the daylight's brightening gleam,
>   On the sunny morning.

> " Crimson foxglove, tall and high,
>   Bowed as though a king went by ;
>   Heather stood up, proud and shy,
>   On the sunny morning.

> " By the streamlet sat we two,
>   Throned among wild hearts'-ease blue,
>   While he said ' Dear, I love you.'
>   Oh, the sunny morning ! "

There came a sudden chillness: we looked up;
Within the doorway stood a figure grand,
A figure worse than horrid hideousness,
For this was horrid beauty. Tall and large,
With womanly dark hair that fell behind
A massive face, deep graven in strong lines
Around the lip and nostril, and the brow,
Where silken lashes, startled, stood upright,
Away from maniac eyes.

            At length she spoke
In sonorous tones, that rolled upon the air
Like church bells tolling 'mid an earthquake's crash :—

" A Prynne can only love a Prynne:
    Doom one.
The Prynne who weds a Prynne, weds Death:
    Doom two.
The Prynne who weds not Death goes mad, like me:
    Doom three."

" Mother !" was all Mark said : long afterwards
I saw his face in death, less rigid, wan.
Beneath his voice she seemed to shrink and fall
Suddenly, to a woman old and weak.

She crept to Agnes, saying, " Nestie, dear ;
Don't you remember how I reared you, Nest ?
Your mother died ; she had the lighter fate."

  " Yes, I remember."
                        Holy, calm, and sweet,
Came Agnes' words, as steals an *Angelus*
Across a battle-field.
                    " What was there wrong,
Was any one unkind ?"

                      " Yes, most unkind :
I had a doll ; oh, such a pretty one !
And it was lost ; they would not help me look."

  " My sister died, an infant ; then this came."
So murmured Mark ; his mother rambled on,
" No one would search, and so I stole away ;
But still I cannot find it ; will you help ?"

  " Yes, we will seek together ; let us go ;
We still may find it in the place you left."
So Agnes spoke, and wound her soft, firm arm
About the feeble, shrinking frame, as though
She fain would heal sick body and sick soul.

"I will come too," said Mark; his mother cried,
"Not him, he looks—as did his father once—
As though he loathed me; no, I will not him."

"I can take care of her," said Agnes, then.

"And who of you?"
                              She smiled, "Oh, I am safe."

"Yes, I forgot; 'tis even as they say,
Seraphs are safe within the jaws of hell."

Mark yielded; but as Agnes turned to go,
She laid her little hand upon his arm
With gentlest touch, and with sweet penitence,
As though she stole some filial right from him,
Said, "Dear, you know it is my mother, too."
So they passed out, bright youth and dreary age;
And as a staircase light fell on them there,
We saw an awful likeness in the pair.

Mark laid his forehead where her hand had lain,
And sighed, as one who sighs out life in pain.
"O God! 'twas this I knew, 'twas this I feared,
To see the trouble grow into her eyes;

E

To see my queen sink lower than the brutes,
And know it was my hand had dragged her down,
And know that I had done it, I, alone !"
Then he arose, and followed afar off.

The daylight waned, and shadows, gaunt and still,
Crept in, and darkly filled my cousins' place,
Until, for cowardice, I cried aloud.
Then Agnes came, and said that all was well,
And shared with me a sudden rain of tears,
Quick dried as thunder showers ; then, like a bird,
That sings its fluttered nestlings into rest,
She softly sang an ancient British hymn :—

" Holy Father, God most tender,
    We, Thy children, cry to Thee ;
  Let Thy light shine through our darkness,
      Till our earth-blind eyes shall see ;
  See the thread that guides our wanderings,
      See the hand that holds us free.
        Holy Father, hear our cry !

" Holy Father, we poor lambkins
    Out of bitter woe do bleat ;
  Strong men drive us o'er the mountains,
      Sharpest stones do pierce our feet,

While before us, and behind us,
　　Dewy grass shines moist and sweet.
　　　Holy Father, hear our cry !

" Holy Father, those Thy servants
　　Who did bring the good news here,
　Said that Thou wast ever with them,
　　That they knew not how to fear;
　Art Thou with us, too, O Father ?
　　Suffer us to feel Thee near.
　　　Holy Father, hear our cry ! "

Mark entered, silently, and listening, stayed
Till she had finished; then he said to her,
" Saint Agnes, my Saint Agnes, shipwrecked men
Grow strangely bold when they cast overboard
That last of anchors, Hope ; until, at length,
Despair might pass for bravery.　So, I
Dare now what I have never dared before,
And pray that you will stoop, before we part,
From your high maidenhood, and kiss me, Sweet."

She stood before him, Ruth-like, meek, and still,
Until between her eyebrows dark and clear
He laid a solemn, sacramental kiss.

E 2

·Part III.

I THINK some strength died out of Mark that night:
  A certain patience grew on him from then,
And quietness, like the calm of dying men.
His journey was delayed from day to day;
The mother died, all suddenly, at last,
He only being with her, and some said
He murdered her; so wicked is the world!
He needs must stay to face the slander down,
Though we, who loved him, cared about it least,
Until I said one eve, "Why, Mark, your hand
Grows thin and pale, and, held up so, looks like
An alabaster shade before a lamp."

  Agnes was painting, but she raised her head,
And turned on him her tender, lustrous eyes
With gaze of woful pity, love, and pain.
He smiled at her as though she reached his wound

And touched it with a touch of anodyne ;
As being healed, he smiled again, and said,
" Sweetheart, you have not sung to me so long ;
They say frogs croak to pique the nightingales
Into melodic contest ; thus croak I :—

A NIGHT-WATCH.

" Woe is my mother that reared me, for I am a man of
strife,
I have not hated my neighbour, and yet he would seek
my life.
Prophets that prophesy smooth things, to them shall
the smooth things come ;
Better than coal from the altar it is that a man be dumb.
Wake her not up, my beloved ; fan her with breeze
of myrrh.

" Happiness is not the one thing a man should essay
to gain,
So I have said with the others, when I had but medium
pain.
Some of the planets, it may be, have air that is pure
and best ;
He who should set out to reach them would need on
the way to rest.

Wake her not up, my beloved. Strange that she
  does not stir !

" Heroes exult in the conflict, and madmen rush forth
  and die.
Neither a hero nor madman—alas for my state!—am I;
Something of clearness of vision doth dawn on my eyes
  from far,
Nothing of clearness of action agrees with the things
  that are.
  Wake her not up, my beloved; pillow the dainty head.

" Life, with its broken endeavours, seems sometimes
  like rotten fruit,
Only the worse for the sunshine of heaven that does
  not suit ;
Plant-like, we need lie in darkness before we translated
  be,
Hades must rest us for ages ere we shall the glory see.
  Wake her not up, my beloved. Merciful God! she
    is dead."

  " Mark, you are ill !" said Agnes suddenly.
He answered low, " No, dear, a little tired,

As a tired child will lean its head against
Its mother's hand, not all for weariness."

Like two pure souls that on their way to earth
Had met in vacuous space, and recognized
Their kinship with a mystic deep delight
And silence eloquent, so these two pierced
Into the spirit depths of either heart,
With solemn joy, and wonderment, and peace,
Unsatisfied with sight, yet gazing still ;
Until a sudden shadow dimmed Mark's eyes.
And Agnes, reading it, saw what he feared
For her, and in her ; and she shrank, like one
All wrongfully accused of leprosy,
Half angered and half sad at such a thought.
I, sorely pressed with pain, sang hurriedly
A baby song which she had taught of old :—

   " All the little flowers lie dead, dead,
     All the little flowers lie dead ;
For the Frost-king came, and he knew no shame,
     And all the little flowers lie dead.

   " All the little birds lie dead, dead,
     All the little birds lie dead ;

For the Man-king came, and he called them game,
   And all the little birds lie dead.

  "All the little stars are dead, dead,
   All the little stars are dead ;
For the Sun-king came, with his daylight flame,
   And all the little stars are dead."

  "A foolish song, but you have Agnes' voice,"
Mark said, and then he drew my lips to his.
Beneath the touch my sleeping woman's soul
Was troubled into life, and I recoiled.

  "What is it?" Agnes asked.   Mark only smiled:
"The child is pettish, Sweet, like all her race ;
We have our special weaknesses, we Prynnes,
Our angers, fantasies, and ghostly fears,
No Saxon courage of tenacity;
We spring, and rush, and suddenly fall back :
Sometimes I almost hate to be a Prynne."

  "Is that, then, us?" I said, amazed, ashamed ;
But Agnes, laying her cheek upon my hair,
Made me a child again.

               All this while
A ceaseless moaning had gone round the house,
A sighing like the sighing of the sea.

A distant gale, Mark said; but as he spoke
It neared, and crashed against the window-frames,
Like some poor mendicant, as Agnes said,
Who fails, with famished voice, to make men hear
Until, Death-driven, he leaps boldly up
And batters at the door until it opes.

Suddenly from the wall a picture sprang,
And fell at Agnes' feet; she smiled, " Poor nun,
I think we will not hang her any more."
Then told me the tradition, how 'twas said
That this had been a weak and foolish Prynne,
Who took the veil, repented it, and died.

" The storm has passed," Mark said; " 'twas
        strangely short.
Listen, how still it is, for you to sing
The plaint I heard at dusk, dear, yester-eve,
Your last new song."

        " My last song, yes,"
And Agnes smiled her danger smile, that thrilled
One's soul, as when a rift in stormy clouds
Shows the blue ether in unearthly calm :—

" I think we have not been impatient, Lord,
    We know Thou lovest us, and we love Thee :
  We hold up chainèd hands before Thee, Lord,
    And only wonder when they will be free.

" A little happiness, good Lord, dear Lord,
    If only for a moment ere we die ;
  Life is so short, yet seems so long with pain.
    ' A moment's bliss' is all our longing cry——"

  She ceased, with catching breath, and cried, " The
    tree !"
Before the house there stood a mountain ash,
Which some far-distant Prynne had brought to share
The changes in the family estate.
Though bent and scarred with age and evil times,
It still upreared its wand-like spears of leaves,
That shimmered silver in the fitful light.

  The storm, returning, had seized hold of this,
'Twas bowed and quivering like a foundering ship,
With mutinous leaves, that whispered cheek on cheek,
How they would help the wrecking wind this night.

E'en as we looked 'twas done : the old tree fell,
Shaking the near foundations of the house,
Till little smoke-like cones of dust arose ;
And then the floor curved upward, so it seemed,
Towards the ceiling, that, on swaying walls,
Went round and round in dizzying circle dim.
" Love !" " Love!" my cousins cried, with out-stretched
      arms,
And flowed together, like two parted streams
Long sundered meeting, meeting at the sea.
Then all was dark.

          When I at length awoke
I heard my father and his brother call :
"The microscope!"—"The telescope!"—"The child!"[1]
And thought of how, 'tis said, old men and babes
Bear anything.

          Stung into sudden life, I rose,
And found my cousins 'neath a fallen beam,
That, falling, sheltered them from all but death ;
Crowned with the roses from the broken vase,
They lay, a sleeping king and queen, at rest.
  Her face, upturned to his, lay on his breast,

COMRADES UNCHOSEN.

" MANY maidens, many minds ;
    He that finds one, seldom binds.
I will never choose my wife as one of many.
    But the maid who stands alone,
    And in solitude has grown,
Such a one I wed, if, truly, I wed any."

    So the stalwart youth did pass,
    Treading down the tender grass,
While a maiden in the group looked shyly after.
    Gentle gaze he could not see,
    But the breezes, wickedly,
Came behind him with the sound of girlish laughter.

" How the mope doth glow'r and grope ! "
    Said a damsel, who had hope
That the glow'ring and the groping were a token,
    Not of love she might return,
    But of love that she would spurn,
When the manly honest words were once out-spoken.

Then the maiden with a soul
Saw her lover reach his goal,
Never turning, turning once to look behind him;
And she said, " He loves his toil,
Loves its constant seam and soil :
They that seek him, with the earth-men still shall find
him."

But an angel, passing by,
Caught the heavy weary sigh
That the wrestler sent across the shoulders near him.
Then he saw the maiden fair
Standing solitary there,
And he knew it was his sin that she did fear him.

Worker fleet and dreamer sweet
Then in blissful rush did meet,
And the root of pain was drawn from out its hiding.
" You had merry company."
" You had comrades rough," said she.
" Borne, not chosen," came from both with gentle
chiding.

AT THE BREACH.

A LL over for me
    The struggle, and possible glory!
   All swept past,
In the rush of my own brigade.
    Will charges instead,
And fills up my place in the story;
    Well,—'tis well,
By the merry old games we played.

There's a fellow asleep, the lout! in the shade of the
    hillock yonder;
What a dog it must be to drowse in the midst of a
    time like this!
Why, the horses might neigh contempt at him; what is
    he like, I wonder?
If the smoke would but clear away, I have strength in
    me yet to hiss.

F

Will, comrade and friend,
We parted in hurry.of battle ;
All I heard
Was your sonorous " Up, my men !"
Soon conquering pæans
Shall cover the cannonade's rattle ;
Then, home bells,
Will you think of me sometimes, then ?

How that rascal enjoys his snooze ! Would he wake
to the touch of powder ?
A reveillé of broken bones, or a prick of a sword might
do.
" Hai, man ! the general wants you ; " if I could but for
once call louder :
There is something infectious here, for my eyelids are
dropping too.

Will, can you recall
The time we were lost on the Bright Down ?
Coming home late in the day,
As Susie was kneeling to pray,
Little blue eyes and white night-gown,

Saying, " Our Father, who art,—
Art what?" so she stayed with a start.
" In Heaven," your mother said softly.
And Susie sighed " So far away !"—
'Tis nearer, Will, now to us all.

It is strange how that fellow sleeps ! stranger still that
    his sleep should haunt me ;
If I could but command his face, to make sure of the
    lesser ill :
I will crawl to his side and see, for what should there
    be there to daunt me ?
What there ? what there ! Holy Father in Heaven,
    not Will !

    Will, dead Will !
Lying here, and I could not feel you !
    Will, brave Will !
Oh, alas, for the noble end !
    Will, dear Will !
Since no love nor remorse could heal you,
    Will, good Will !
Let me die on your breast, old friend !

THE OLD ASTRONOMER.

REACH me down my Tycho Brahé,—I would
    know him when we meet,
When I share my later science, sitting humbly at his
    feet;
He may know the law of all things, yet be ignorant of
    how
We are working to completion, working on from then
    till now.

Pray, remember, that I leave you all my theory com-
    plete,
Lacking only certain data, for your adding, as is
    meet;
And remember, men will scorn it, 'tis original and
    true,
And the obloquy of newness may fall bitterly on you.

But, my pupil, as my pupil you have learnt the worth
    of scorn ;
You have laughed with me at pity, we have joyed to
    be forlorn ;
What, for us, are all distractions of men's fellowship
    and smiles ?
What, for us, the goddess Pleasure, with her meretri-
    cious wiles ?

You may tell that German college that their honour
    comes too late.
But they must not waste repentance on the grizzly
    savant's fate ;
Though my soul may set in darkness, it will rise in
    perfect light ;
I have loved the stars too truly to be fearful of the night.

What, my boy, you are not weeping ? You should
    save your eyes for sight ;
You will need them, mine observer, yet for many
    another night.
I leave none but you, my pupil, unto whom my plans
    are known.
You "have none but me," you murmur, and I "leave
    you quite alone " ?

Well then, kiss me,—since my mother left her blessing
  on my brow,
There has been a something wanting in my nature
  until now ;
I can dimly comprehend it,—that I might have been
  more kind,
Might have cherished you more wisely, as the one I
  leave behind.

I "have never failed in kindness"? No, we lived too
  high for strife,—
Calmest coldness was the error which has crept into
  our life ;
But your spirit is untainted, I can dedicate you still
To the service of our science : you will further it ? you
  will !

There are certain calculations I should like to make
  with you,
To be sure that your deductions will be logical and
  true ;
And remember, " Patience, Patience," is the watch-
  word of a sage,
Not to-day nor yet to-morrow can complete a perfect
  age.

I have sown, like Tycho Brahé, that a greater man
    may reap ;
But if none should do my reaping, 'twill disturb me in
    my sleep.
So be careful and be faithful, though, like me, you
    leave no name ;
See, my boy, that nothing turn you to the mere pursuit
    of fame.

I must say Good-bye, my pupil, for I cannot longer
    speak ;
Draw the curtain back for Venus, ere my vision grows
    too weak :
It is strange the pearly planet should look red as fiery
    Mars,—
God will mercifully guide me on my way amongst the
    stars.

SLEIGHING SONG.

OVER the frozen snow,
  With a musical swish we go ;
Never a planet that rolls in space
Doth travel more smoothly his destined race,
  Or less of the earth doth know.

  Covered all carking care,
  With a robe of the frost-work fair ;
We are the creatures of joy to-day,
As free as the feathers that round us play,
  The flakes of the crystal air.

  Swimming the wind are we,
  Like the fish in the buoyant sea ;
Never a gambol in deepest ocean
Could equal our subtle delight of motion,
  Nor thrill with a purer glee.

Clouds overhead, you say?
And a glooming of ashen grey?
Let it come down on us, swift and strong,
The morrow be dreary, and dark, and long—
It cannot destroy this day.

OUT OF DARKNESS INTO LIGHT.

WE have travelled through the darkness,
  Thou and I, for many days;
Till we wondered at the sunshine,
  When at length we felt its rays.

Chill and lonely was the pathway,
  Only lighted by the snow,
With the cutting east wind only
  To declare how we should go.

On our right, the frozen river,
  Where the drownèd lay asleep;
On our left, the rocky mountain,
  So precipitously steep;

All around the gloomy shadows
  Of the failures gone before;
While the leafless branches whispered,
  We should do no less, no more.

We should falter and should stumble,
  And should fail to reach the end ;
And should die in the beginning—
  Die together, O my friend !

Die together ?—'twas a jewel
  Which they threw us, for a stone :
Come what might, we could remember
  That we should not be alone ;

So, with hands entwined the closer,
  We pressed on against the blast ;
And we bided for the daylight,
  And the daylight came at last.

First, the darkness grew to blackness,
  And we shivered in the cold ;
And we trembled, lest our fingers
  Should not keep their faithful hold ;

Then a strange grey veil fell on us,—
  Was it darkness ? was it light ?
And we questioned each, " What is it ?
  Coming day, or coming night ? "

Then upon the far horizon
   Came the faintest tint of gold ;
Then the cloud became a glory,
   And the mystery was told ;

Richer, deeper, grew the radiance,
   Till our eyes could hold no more.
We had travelled to the eastward,
   And our journeying was o'er.

Now the light is round about us,
   And the sun to guide our feet ;
And along the mountain pathway
   Shine the flowers, pale and sweet ;

And we pluck us each a blossom
   To remind us as we go,
How we went, we two together,
   Through the darkness and the snow ;

And, whate'er may be the friendships
   We may gain in after years,
None can come between the compact
   Which has been annealed by tears.

OMÀR AND THE PERSIAN.

THE victor stood beside the spoil, and by the
    grinning dead :
"The land is ours, the foe is ours, now rest, my men,"
    he said.
But while he spoke there came a band of foot-sore,
    panting men :
"The latest prisoner, my lord, we took him in the
    glen,
And left behind dead hostages that we would come
    again."

The victor spoke: "Thou, Persian dog! hast cost
    more lives than thine.
That was thy will, and thou shouldst die full thrice, if
    I had mine.

Dost know thy fate, thy just reward?"   The Persian
    bent his head,

" I know both sides of victory, and only grieve," he
    said,

" Because there will be none to fight 'gainst thee when
    I am dead.

" No Persian faints at sight of Death, we know his face
    too well,—

He waits for us on mountain side, in town, or shelter'd
    dell;

But I crave a cup of wine, thy first and latest boon,

For I have gone three days athirst, and fear lest I may
    swoon,

Or even wrong mine enemy, by dying now, too soon."

The cup was brought; but ere he drank, the Persian
    shudder'd white.

Omàr replied, " What fearest thou?   The wine is clear
    and bright;

We are no poisoners, not we, nor traitors to a guest,

No dart behind, nor dart within, shall pierce thy
    gallant breast;

Till thou hast drained the draught, O foe, thou dost in
    safety rest."

The Persian smiled, with parchèd lips, upon the foe-
men round,
Then poured the precious liquid out, untasted, on the
ground.
"Till that is drunk, I live," said he, "and while I live,
I fight ;
So, see you to your victory, for 'tis undone this night ;
Omàr the worthy, battle fair is but thy god-like right."

Upsprang a wrathful army then,—Omàr restrained
them all,
Upon no battle-field had rung more clear his martial
call,
The dead men's hair beside his feet as by a breeze was
stirr'd,
The farthest henchman in the camp the noble man-
date heard :
"Hold ! if there be a sacred thing, it is the warrior's
word."

STUDENT FRIENDS.

I.

FRANK, I had left you, lost you,
  Drowned in the rush of days;
All the old time was ended,
  Blurred with a twilight haze.

Only I knew, with you, Frank,
  Somewhere the world was blessed—
Blessed with a spirit steadfast,
  Soul that my youth loved best.

Thus I was biding softly,
  Mining my way to light;
Hewing the tough old problems,
  Working for day through night.

But all my mine exploded—
  Came there a tale so base ;
You for the pseudo hero !
  Dark grew your pictured face.

You to be living vilely,
  Hampered with hidden sin !—
Send me a full denial,
  That I may your victory win.

II.

True ! and you cannot help me,
  Cannot explain the thing ?
Will not come near from henceforth,
  Lest you the taint should bring ?

I must forgive, renounce you,
  Leave you to go your way ?
That your reply, my brother ?
  Woe on this evil day !

Were you not real of old, then?
  He whom I knew as Frank
Could not have sunk so deeply,
  Could not have grown so rank.

Was it the deadly nightshade,
  Worn as my boyhood's flower?
Was I a dreamer dreaming,
  Held in a falsehood's power?

Is there a sun in heaven?
  Is there a God on high?
All my old world is shattered ;
  Brother, good-bye, good-bye.

III.

Frank, I have heard the story,
  Pitiful, strange, and sweet ;
All that you would not tell me—
  All of your grand defeat.

Not without sin, O brother,
  Hast thou come forth alone ;
But who am I to judge thee ?
  How should I cast a stone ?

Wounded and smirched with battle,
  Righting thy soul at last ;
Would I had fought beside thee !—
  Oh for the danger past !

I am the meaner now, friend ;
  Say, canst thou stoop to me ?
Thou, with thy crown of suffering—
  Thou who by right art free.

Wilt thou receive me, brother ?
  Thou art the teacher now :
Life has grown strangely sacred,
  Low at thy feet I bow.
There is a hidden conflict,—
  Thorns for the victor's brow.

YEOMAN SERVICE.

IS it death, is it death, that is coming? Well, let it
    come:
It has been, like "The French!" but a cry of
    "Wolf!" for so long,
That I think I am glad now at last to find it is here,
That the enemy stands at the door. Walk in, tardy foe.

When the minister came from Bethesda after my
    soul,
He declared I was Pagan in strength, it grieved him
    to say.
"Are the Christians all weak, then?" I asked: "if so,
    none for me;"
Let the women be meek, but the men must stand till
    they die.

Holy Father, forgive me! I am but sore angered with
    these;
I am Thine, as Thou knowest, Thine alone,—never
    bended my knees
To the Pope, nor the Saints, nor the Virgin; nor
    cowered to please
The young parson in yellow, who moans at the Chapel
    of Ease.

I know naught about singing and playing, nor wearing
    of crowns;
But there may be a school outside Heaven for learn-
    ing such things,
Or the Master may give me employment I know how
    to do,—
Say the care of the wondrous white horses of John the
    Divine.

Or I might keep the gates 'gainst the dogs of the liars
    without,—
I am great against liars myself; yet I lied to the squire
When I met him, along with the rest, at his coming of
    age,
And hurra'd for "Our noble young master"—he,
    mean as a hound!

And again, when the parson I spoke of came here
　　t'other day,—
Out of church he is gentle, and pure as a woman, and
　　poor,
And the poverty is such a kingship, becomes him so
　　well,
That I called him " Your Reverence " humbly : I doubt
　　it was wrong.

There's another sin, too, on my conscience : when we
　　were first wed,
I was jealous with Janet, miscalled her a sinner one
　　day,
And I struck her ! She lives with the angels this many
　　a year ;
But I'll scarce dare to meet her, till Thou, Lord, hast
　　spoke to her first.

I would fain make confession to Thee, Lord, before I
　　come hence ;
But the children crowd round me with crying, and
　　harass my soul.

If they would but be still for a moment until I am
    gone,
And not thrust in their sighing while I am at talk with
    the King.

Well, what is it you want, then, Kezia? speak quickly,
    my girl!
" Say good-bye to us, father; nor mutter like this, in
    your sleep."
Little lass! she is tender and fair, and the boys are
    good boys;
I must help them from yonder. Good-bye, lass! Good-
    bye, boys, Good-bye!

SHIPWRECK.

THREE days and nights the boat stood out,
    And battled for its life ;
" We'll win through yet," the captain said,
    And buckled to the strife.

We cheered him then, a feeble cheer,
    There was no breath to spare ;
For one hand held a fainting hope,
    And one a strong despair.

The sun went down behind the hills,
    The mighty hills of foam ;
And as the green the crimson caught,
    We thought of hills at home.

And here and there a sigh went up
  That might have been a prayer ;
There was no time for talking then,
  No place for weakness there.

Then, like a mighty ghost, arose
  The darkness of the night,—
Came on and on, close after us,
  Pursued and slew the light.

We drifted on, and on, and on,
  We knew not how nor where ;
And as the chill of morning came
  We scarcely seemed to care.

Only the captain cheered us still:
  "'Tis darkness tries a man ;
Fair-weather sailors are not we ;
  Let him despair who can."

And then our dying hope sprang up,
  Like lion from its lair ;
It caught the traitor, Fear, and slew,
  And left us strong to bear.

The daylight came; we sighted land;
   The captain bared his head :
" I said we would win through, my men ; "
   And then he fell back dead.

We gained the land right speedily ;
   It was an island fair ;
But 'twas a sad ship's company
   Came off, and left him there.

SWINGING THE CENSER.

Christmas Morning.

I.

BROTHER WITHIN THE CHANCEL.

GATHER his robes about him,
  Follow the priestly feet ;
Choke him with fragrant incense,
  Nothing shall purge him sweet.
Mean to his inmost fibre,
  Blushing not, soul nor cheek ;
He is the holy Father,
  We are his servants meek.

Fitting his fingers neatly,
  Joint upon flaccid joint ;
Playing with hand and eyebrow,
  He whom the saints anoint.

Bowing like one decrepid,
   Wailing as one forlorn;
Would it were skull, not tonsure,
   That from his brain was shorn!

Credo—non possum, Father.
   Kyrie—not for me:
Gloria—poor excelsis!
   Sanctus—if I were free!
Gather his garments deftly,
   Follow him soft and still;
Envy and hate confess I,
   Will he absolve? he will.
There is a slothful patience,
   Brutishness passeth skill.

II.

SISTER OUTSIDE THE CHANCEL.

Close to the Reverend Father!
   Well to be Leon this day!
Think of me, brother, my brother,
   And for thy sister pray.

It is so hard to be trustful,
  Trusting for daily bread;
Only the birds and the angels
  Are without storehouse fed.

What if I sin, never knowing?
  Jesu, forgive, I pray;
Mother of Jesu, keep near me,
  Dark is the way.
O miserere nobis,
  Domine!

III.

CHILD IN THE CHOIR.

Unto us a Child is born,
Unto us a Son is given;
Wonderful, the Counsellor,
  The Prince of Peace.
More than they who watch for morn,
Have the blind and weary striven;

Yet He waiteth evermore.
They who ask have all things given ;
   Light shall increase.
   Gloria in excelsis Deo !
      Amen.

IV.

BELLS IN THE DISTANCE.

Farther from the priest,
   Nearer those that pray ;
Farther from the lamps,
   Nearer light of day.
Yet where prayer is made
   God is wont to stay.
Through, not past, the church
   Is the appointed way.
      Pax vobiscum.
      Amen.

"DISCHARGED HONOURABLY."

NANCY, old woman, I want you ;
    Come to my side and spin :
I can hear the reel of your whirring wheel
    More than the farm-yard din.

I " must spin also," my mistress ?
    Wind you a soldier's yarn ?
'Tis a wondrous whirl of a life, my girl—
    Many a hole to darn.

Many a field has been foughten
    More for the fight's own sake,
Than for the vict'ry gained, or a flag unstained,
    Or for a cause at stake.

And I have seen, in the battle,
　　Men who were staunch and true,
Yet who turned aside when the foeman died,
　　Groaning for him they slew.

And, as I sit here and ponder,
　　Living the whole again,
I have sometimes thought, Which is dearest bought—
　　Victor's or vanquished's pain?

But if the doubting had come, Nance,
　　When I was called to fight;
I had parleyed not, but mine own good shot
　　Should have struck home outright.

None should have had it against me
　　That I had turned aside,
When the rear pressed on, and the front had gone,
　　Or, as some phrased it, died.

Now, as I puzzle it over,
　　Something a truth reveals,
That the soul is fed by its daily bread,
　　Owes but the debt it feels.

And, as the General gave us
    Only our part to do,
'Tis enough to know we have wrought it so
    That it shall prove us true.

If I were scholar to word it,
    Were not so dull of speech,
'Tis a gladsome thought, that no soul is taught
    More than its power can reach.

Thinking is thirsty, my woman ;
    Reach me the cider down.
If the parson sweats when a thought he gets,
    Well he may dwine and frown.

DIED YESTERDAY.

DEAD ! Roger the true, dearest and noblest of all
    men ;
Ruler and helper and guide; my brother and friend in
    one.
Roger, it is not like you, leaving me here in the battle :
Did you not say you would fight—I, sing when the
    strife was done ?
How can I sing, O Roger, since thus is the conflict
    won ?

Surely I need you, brother, more than they need you
    in heaven,—
They who have all things good, and I who had only
    you ;
How shall I live without you, hardening, old, and
    lonely ?
Nobody cares, as you cared, what manner of things I do.
What if you should not know me, at last when we meet,
    we two ?

Truly, I must grow duller, or die like a severed
    branchlet,—
Dying is coming to you, and ending the story sad ;
Only the sickness of grief lingers so long in its killing ;
Shall I, by instinct, forget the brightness my days once
    had ?
Learn like a flower to sleep, or, bird-like, be lightly
    glad ?

Save me from that, O Roger ! keep me alive to
    sorrow ;
Human, by birthright of pain, and free of the guild
    of woe ;
Tender, by thorns in the heart, so that our kindred
    may trust me ;
Dropping not gall, but balm, as you did, wherever
    I go ;
Oh, let me meet you worthy, though swift come the
    time, or slow.

"BETTER A LIVING DOG THAN A DEAD LION."

NO, no, no; let the curs that leap yelping around him
Bay out their feeble anger; the monarch has death for state.
Hunted and wounded and slain, let him lie where the trackers have found him,
With the thorns that he fell on in dying pressed into his leonine breast,
With the undergrowth closing above him, a shroud for the king in his rest.

No, no, no; though his reign may be broken and ended,
King in his life he was, and in death he is kingly still.
What though his subjects have fled, though he lieth untended, unfriended?

With the grandeur of loneliness died he, with anguish
    trode under his feet;
'Twas the climax of life when he yielded, 'twas victory
    writ in defeat.

No, no, no; by the greatness not on him, but in him,
Ruled he in robes of might, with his nature for
    brightest crown.
Never a tiger nor snake to their banquet of foulness
    could win him;
All unconscious of evil, he shunned it with haughtiness
    greater than pride;
By the lofty ideal he left us, 'tis good he thus lived,
    and thus died.

THE COAST-GUARD'S STORY.

OUT on the isle of Mona,
  Mona with rocks so red,
For the sins of the wreckers who preyed there once,
  So the tradition said,

There lived a sturdy coast-guard,
  Watching the whole night long;
And he sang to the sea, to the sea sang he,
  This was his simple song: —

" Only over the sea,
  Only over the sea !
There my love doth dwell, she that loves me well,
  Waiting and looking for me."

Singing away the darkness,
　　　Unto the dawning white,
When the sea-gulls came screaming " A - i - e. 'Tis day!"
　　　Bats shivered " Woe for night!"

Out of the waning darkness,
　　　Driven before the sun,
A ship came drifting, and drifting fast,
A ship with never a sail nor mast,
　　　All of its voyage done.

The coast-guard waited with hands fast clenched,
　　　Visage a purple white,
" Something is here that I needs must fear,
　　　After my dream last night."

The ship came closer, the skeleton ship—
　　　Tangle of shattered ropes,
　　　Fragments of scattered hopes,
　　　Did round its timbers cling;
Among the shrouds, in a hammock of wreck,
　　　A dead man's form did swing.

The coast-guard sprang with his heavy strength,
    And bore the body down;
He drew it in to a tomb-like rock,—
    The dead man seemed to frown.

The ship went curtseying back to sea,
    Like one whose task was done;
The coast-guard stood, in a daze stood he,
    Before the blinding sun.

Of all he rescued from out the sea
    He saw one hand alone;
On all the hand he could only see
    One well-remembered stone.

    "O ring!" the coast-guard cried,
    "How hast thou come to this?
The ring I gave her, my promised bride,
    With many a tear and kiss?

    "Man, didst thou slay my wife?
    Though thou wert three times dead
I would avenge her, would claim thy life
    For each dear hair of her head.

"Or did she give my ring?
  How could such vileness be?
Man, with the truth at your black false heart,
  Declare it now to me!"—
The dead man smiled with an awful calm,
  And not a word said he.

"If she be false! O God,
  Thou who the truth canst tell."—
The coast-guard swayed like a tree up-torn,
  And on his knees he fell.

He grasped the fingers stiff,
  And loosed them one by one;
The dead man's hand was a faithful hand,
  Its work was nearly done.

A letter, held till now,
  Dropped from the open palm;
The case was sealed with the coast-guard's name—
  He read in dream-like calm.

"Love," so it ran, "I am writing,
  Writing our last Good-bye;

I send the ring by a trusty hand,
    For they say I must die, must die.

" Do not be broken-hearted,
    Lover so true, so dear ;
The pain is nothing,—I think of you,
    And I know that you fain were here.

" But you must hold your post, dear,
    Must not be ruined for me ;
Before my letter can reach you, love,
    I shall see you across the sea.

" Only a little while, dear,
    You will be free, be free !
We two shall meet on the golden street,
    In the city that knows no sea.
      Love, true love !
Be happy, not sad, for me."

The letter dropt from his palsied hand,
Two men lay stretched on the shifting strand ;
Like brothers lay, in a close embrace,
The cold sea-spray on each pale, pale face.

But the one to whom living meant only pain,
Was the one to be laden with life again.

Many a year has vanished ;
        Grey is the coast-guard now,
With a shadowy smile in his tender eyes,
        Strength on his patient brow.

Still at his work he paces,
        Watching the whole night long ;
And the birds, his companions, asleep on high,
        Hear not his passionate song.

" Only over the sea,
        Only over the sea !
There my love doth dwell, she that loves me well,
        Waiting and looking for me."

THE ROUNDHEAD'S CHAUNT.

THOUGH the way may be long,
    Though the wicked may be strong,
God is stronger, and eternity is longer.
    Though great Cromwell be dead,
    And with him our mighty head,
Wise and tender is the Lord, our one Defender.

    Though the weak may fall off,
    Though the shallow hearts may scoff,
We are better'd, for without them are less fetter'd.
    When the keen searching breeze
    Sweeps the dead leaves from the trees,
Then revealed stands the strength before concealed.

Let us be, we are free
Of the joys of life, for we
Do not flout them, though we choose to live
without them.
There is hope for the brave,
There is joy beyond the wave,
Which, in breaking, will but bear us past forsaking.

FRUITION.

WHAT is it you say, little Grace, that my picture
    is famous?
Well, the thing was a true thing, and so I am glad 'tis
    acknowledged;
And the truth was wrought in me, and therefore 'twas
    mine to declare it:
For the rest, it may go, with the toy that we shattered
    last even.

Is it well to be clever? you question, my daughter.
    I know not;
I have never been clever myself, only patient and
    faithful,—
Giving out, as a lamp might, the light that was kindled
    within me;
Neither kindling nor radiance mine own, only mine
    was the burning.

In my youth I was vainer, as though only I had a
   message,
And the error men saw would be vanquished the
   moment they saw it.
I was young and so happy, my child, that I revelled in
   sadness,
And men said of this painter, " He gives us the black-
   ness of darkness."

But the shadows came on me; your mother, your
   grandmother, faded,
And the angel shone through her more brightly, and
   burnt to my soul.
And I painted her, feature by feature, my love, in her
   dying !
And I thought, Was I human or demon, to study
   her so ?

And she died as the picture was finished ; my darling,
   my darling !
But from out of the distance came murmurings, mel
   lowed by time :

"God be thanked, for this vision He gives us, of
sweetness and glory."
Then I knew that the work was not mine, that in
truth 'twas well done.

Then the sorrow of life made my righteousness softer,
more tender ;
I grew careless of preaching, cared only for healing
men's souls ;
And I painted the flowers by the wayside, and knelt
as I painted ;
And men said, " He is growing, this painter,—is near-
ing the great."

As the racer is cheered in his strife by a voice that he
knows not,
So a friend, who was only a voice to me, led me till
now :
But they say he is dead ; and they praise me, you say,
little Gracie ?
Do they praise him, I wonder, who made me—the
last of my friends ?
Yes, the work is completed, I think, for the worker is
worn.

THE HERMIT.

O UT in the greenwood free,
  Lord of myself to be !
Far from the fuming and fretting of men.—
Surely the father was feeble then :
  " This be your penance," said he.

All the day long mine own,
  Never a jarring tone ;
Now shall I sing as a friar should sing,
Now to the altar pure incense shall bring,
  Living for worship alone.

Come to me, beasts so fair ;
  Flourish, ye flow'rets rare,—
All the creation is perfect but man ;
He is the outlaw, and lives under ban,
  Poisons the innocent air.

Mother, mine earth, be kind ;
Let me, on you reclined,
Dream out my folly, my sin, and my pain ;
Rise as a plant newly bathed with the rain,
Fresh with the fanning of wind.

Fountain so still, so clear,
Let me stoop down and hear
All of the wisdom that babbles so sweet ;
Hast thou no welcome the stranger to greet ?
Hast thou thy secrets, held dear ?

Life, like an autumn day,
Fruitful, shall glide away,
Rich with the wisdom of birds and of bees,
Sweet with the fragrance of blossoming trees,
Bright with the dragon-flies gay.

Glorious life, and good !
Nightshade, be thou monk's hood,
Moss for my pillow and rock for my wall ;
Hunted of many, but hidden from all,
Safe in the sheltering wood.

II.

Mine eyes are heavy with watching,
　My tongue for speech doth thirst;
If only the veriest dog of a man
　Would break this void accurst!

The deer come grazing before me,
　As though a stone were I;
The hare with the scorn of a fear overthrown
　Goes lightly glancing by.

The wood is busy with music,
　The birds in chorus sing;
The adders creep out, and the toads come about,
　As round a vanquished king.

A vision haunts me, and haunts me,
　A dream of tender eyes;
I call her my saint, and I kneel at her shrine,
　But earthly thoughts will rise.

'Tis not Madonna, the Jewess,
　Who died so long ago;
But Mary, the living, that smiles from my wall,—
　The painter wrought it so.

'Tis not the enemy, Satan,
  My gargoyle, carved in wood ;
But Brother Anselmo, the cunning, the base,
  Who all my deeds withstood.

'Tis " Oh for a change in the spectres ! "
  My reeling soul doth sigh.
Ho ! churl of a forester, welcome, my friend !
  God sent you passing by.

III.

God, it is just, though 'tis bitter,
  That I should come to lie,
Lonely and dry as a severed branch,
  Here in my wood to die.

Yet hast Thou shown me Thy mercy :
  Out of the herbs obscure
Many a simple my hands have culled,
  Many an ill to cure.

Now, by so much as I served them,
  Count I my brethren kin ;
Now, by so much as they loved me, Lord,
  Let me Thy pardon win.

Evil my life, and an error,
　Based on a pride so blind,
Deeming that man, of Thy works alone,
　Flourished without his kind.

Now, but for thee, O my Father,
　I had been like the king
Who as a brute with the brutes did graze,
　Sunk to a meaner thing.

Saved by a hand's-breadth from madness —
　Saved, but all useless now,—
Let me be warning who may not guide,
　Publish my latest vow.

All of my life that remaineth,
　Though but a breath it be,
Take it, my brothers, forsaken, lost,
　Take it, as all of me.

BROTHERS.

I STAND outside the Abbey where we stood
      Singing our parts.
'Twas early morning, and our life was good,
      So young our hearts!

Lonely upon the wall one shadow falls —
      Mine, all alone;
Broken, my voice, all inharmonious, calls
      Its other tone.

The city crowd goes past me, rushing by,
      With far-off roar;
Beside my feet the quiet gravestones lie,
      Unseen before.

The windows, all a glory from within,
      Are dull without;
A vision as of death in pain and sin
      Doth glide about.

Arthur, I left you robed in white, and gay,
      A chorister.
Silent I find you,—I so old, and grey,
      And sinister.

Which is my brother? Arthur, dead, a child?
      What kin are we?
Or the bright angel, dwelling undefiled,
      More strange is he.

No friend least known, no foe most held in fear,
      Could scare me so
As could my brother, held familiar, dear,
      So long ago.

Yet as I love him still, though grown so great,
      It well may be
His love doth bridge the gulf between our state,
      And reach to me.

QUESTIONINGS.

IS IT SO, O CHRIST IN HEAVEN?

"I have yet many things to say unto you, but ye cannot bear them now."—St. John xvi. 12.

IS it so, O Christ in heaven, that the souls we loved
    so well
Must remain in pain eternal, must abide in endless
    hell?
And our love avail them nothing, even Thine avail
    no more?
Is there nothing that can reach them,—nothing bridge
    the chasm o'er?—
" I have many things to tell you, but ye cannot bear
    them now."

Is it so, O Christ in heaven, that the Antichrist must
    reign?
Still assuming shapes Protean, dying but to live
    again?

Waging war on God Almighty, by destroying feeble
    man,
With the heathen for a rear-guard, and the learnèd for
    the van ?—
" I have many things to tell you, but ye cannot bear
    them now."

Is it so, O Christ in heaven, that the highest suffer
    most ?
That the strongest wander farthest, and more hope-
    lessly are lost ?
That the mark of rank in nature is capacity for pain,
And the anguish of the singer makes the sweetness of
    the strain ?—
" I have many things to tell you, but ye cannot bear
    them now."

Is it so, O Christ in heaven, that whichever way
    we go
Walls of darkness must surround us, things we would
    but cannot know ?

That the Infinite must bound us, as a temple veil
    unrent,
While the Finite ever wearies, so that none attain
    content ?—
" I have many things to tell you, but ye cannot bear
    them now."

Is it so, O Christ in heaven, that the fulness yet to
    come
Is so glorious and so perfect, that to know would strike
    us dumb ?
That, if only for a moment, we could pierce beyond
    the sky
With these poor dim eyes of mortals, we should just
    see God and die ?—
" I have many things to show you, but ye cannot bear
    them now."

DEFEAT.

M^Y darling, O my darling! with the soft sad eyes,
    Set like twilight planets in the raining skies ;
With the brow all patience, and the lips all pain,
Save the curves for kisses—kiss me, love, once again.

My priestess, O my priestess! with the almond bough
That her pale hand holdeth, dry and barren now ;
With its crown of blossoms by the rude wind rent,
With the gift God-taken that of God was sent.

Mine empress, O mine empress! with the shattered
    throne,
Is there yet no kingdom we can call thine own ?
Is success the only thing the world holds good ?
Or is God as man, and could not, if He would ?

No, no, by all the martyrs, and the dear dead Christ ;
By the long bright roll of those whom joy enticed
With her myriad blandishments, but could not win,
Who would fight for victory, but would not sin.

By these, our elder brothers, who have gone before,
And have left their trail of light upon our shore,
We can see the glory of a seeming shame,
We can feel the fulness of an empty name.

Has God become enfeebled in His old, old age ?
Must the whole creation take our narrow gauge ?
Are there no deep thunders which we cannot hear ?
Does the star cease shining when it shines not here ?

No, no, we know, dead Knowledge, that it is not so,
And we feel, dull Feeling, that our souls must grow ;
As the tree feels light, and as the earth feels rain,
So we live till morning :—kiss me, love, once again.

"SORROW AND SIGHING SHALL FLEE
AWAY."—THE PROPHET ISAIAH.

SORROW and sighing, sorrow and sighing,
　　How can it happen that these should pass
Out of a world where the flowers lie dying,
　　Out of a world where all flesh is grass?
Sorrow and sighing, sorrow and sighing,
Dear as the autumn, and fair as the rain.

Sorrow and sighing, sorrow and sighing,
　　Will they then cease, and our souls grow dull?
Sluggishly somnolent, torpidly lying,
　　Lapped in the calm of a deep sea lull?
Sorrow and sighing, sorrow and sighing,--
Should we not long for the thundering main?

Sorrow and sighing, sorrow and sighing,
 All to be done, and our tears gone dry ;
Never a thought o'er the boundary flying,
 Never a grasp as the clouds swing by.
Sorrow and sighing, sorrow and sighing,
All faded out, nothing left to restrain.

Sorrow and sighing, sorrow and sighing,
 What would our days be cut off from these ?
If, at the fairy mart, we were life buying,
 Should we not choose them, past things that please ?
Sorrow and sighing, sorrow and sighing,—
Take what you will, only leave us our pain.

K

SISTERS STILL.

DO you remember, ay, love, even now,
    How by the wintry fire we used to sit
Reclining on the many-coloured rug?
   We were good children always, so they said.
Too good, alas! we had been better worse;
But being as we were, were happy so,
With "Tell me, now, what in the fire you see?"
  "I see a mountain and a burning lake."
  "You mean a burning mountain and a lake?"
  "No, no, a mountain and a burning lake;
The lake where Sodom and Gomorrah burn,
And all the people in them burn and burn,
And then, and now, and evermore they burn."
  "But that is dreadful: God is not like that;
He says 'enough' sometimes."

"You say so, you!
What private knowledge have you?"

Thus we clashed
In sudden steelly war; and all the while
Our placid dolls lay smiling in our laps;
And, like two warring mothers, each would clasp
Her waxen babe, and press its face to hers,
And say, "You are not frightened, are you, Sweet?
We mean no harm, you know, we're often thus."
And in the soft caressing, wrath went out,
And heart drew near to heart with clinging hands:
There followed then, "Dear, it is your turn now:
There is a cavern; tell me what you see."

"I see a silver palace in the sun,
With rose-leaf windows, and an emerald floor,
Where gossamer fairies ever dance and play,
And love, but not too sorely, lest they die."

"The simpletons! to shrink from death or grief:
Why, everybody dies; and as for grief,
When I am old I mean to count my griefs,
And say, 'This have I gained, and this, and this,'
And hold them jewels, as the Bible says,
To give the King."

K 2

Ah, love, love, love ! all die, but not together ;
And they who stay behind, to count such gems,
Grow dizzy, over-laden, over rich.—
But still at even-time we walk together,
And still our souls repose in one Our Father.

IN TIME OF DOUBT.

IF we but had the right
    Sure on our side, and strong ;
Then the soldier should fight with might,
    And the singer should chant his song.
But there cometh a whisper, like whisper of Fate,
"They that conquer the weak are not valiant nor
    great."

If it were ours to view
    Only the half of life ;
If a film on our eyes there grew,
    Then we, blinded, were fit for strife ;
But the heavenly light showeth piercingly clear
That the dwarf in the distance is giant when near.

If it were just to-day
    That we did live and die ;
If our doing would pass away,
    When our power in the grave did lie ;
But we know that the dust in the wheel-tracks of time
Is retarding, or helping, a progress sublime.

If we could calmly rise
    Just for a moment's breath,
To the height of the clear blue skies,
    To the level of life—and death ;
But the anger within us, the anger without,
Ever stirring our zeal, hold it molten in doubt.

FAINT HEART.

WHY was I born, ye angels? was it well?
    Ye might have killed me, such a little thing!
And I had been in Heaven all this while,
  And missed mine heritage of suffering.
Would it have been a loss?   I cannot tell;
    God knows.

Why cry and moan? what matters anything?
  Why vex the quiet air with vain complaints?
The army of immortals marches on,
  And must not tarry, though one, footsore, faints;
Would it be better if another stayed?
    God knows.

What if I died? the world is over full;
  Stronger and better souls would come instead.
Is there no place in Heaven yet for me?
  Must I keep on, with feignèd martial tread?
Live to fear death, and count my sorrow sin?
      God knows.

DOMINE DIRIGE NOS.

GOD is not importunate:
   If we will not hear His voice,
He is silent, and withdraws,
   Angels mourn, and fiends rejoice.
     O Lord, direct us!

Was it our fault Adam fell?
   Did we will his sinning?
Fore-ordained to endless Hell,
   Heaven not for our winning.
     O Lord, direct us!

Other life we know not yet;
   But from what we know of this,
'Tis an evil thing to get:
   Souls unborn come nearest bliss.
     O Lord, direct us!

Darkness, dumbness, fall on us,
  Through the valley groping;
Drowning brothers call on us;
  Some men talk of hoping.
    O Lord, direct us!

DEPARTED.

I LAY down upon my bed,
   With a somewhat aching head,
  And mine eyes disposed for tears :
News of death had come that day,
Of a kinsman far away,
Who had shared my childhood's play :
  And one word rang in mine ears,—
                    Departed !

Back on all my thoughts it came,
Answering to every name,
  Every feeling, grave or gay,
Every picture dark or bright—
As the hours marched through the night.
Till the word seemed like a sprite
  I could neither soothe nor lay :
                    Departed !

Then, since effort seemed in vain,
My resolve began to wane,
   And I let it have its way;
Bade it tell me why I sighed,
Since the dead are glorified;
And for answer it replied,
   "One thing only I can say,
          Departed!"

Other forms its might did show,
Those belovèd long ago,
   Loved and lost, and gone away.
Over all my vision ranged,
Some forgotten, some estranged,
Some still lost, although unchanged.
   Over all still rang the lay,
          Departed!

Then I cried, " In pity show
Something gone,—I wish to go;"
   And I saw how every day
Seems to set the soul more free,
Loose its burdens tenderly—
And the sorrow crushing me
   Hath entirely passed away,
          Departed!

Thus, in merciful relief,
Time's soft hand laid on our grief
  Takes its poignancy away ;
Saves the spirit from despair,
Lightens every load of care,
Till we cease its weight to bear :
  And of us, too, men shall say,
            " Departed ! "

GROWTH.

I.

A LONELY rock uprose above the sea,
   The coral insects fretting at its base ;
And no man came unto its loneliness,
   The very storm-birds shunned its evil case.
Only the ocean beat upon its breast,
   Only the ocean gave it close embrace.

II.

An island was upheaved towards the skies,
   A central fire within its heart had burst :
The rock became a mountain, stern and strong,
   Only the desolation shewed at first ;
A stray bird dropped a seed that fructified,
   No longer reigned the barrenness accursed.

III. ,

A little world stood out among the seas,
    With singing brooks and many a fragrant wood,
Where lovers heard again their story sweet,
    And truth grew fair, more fully understood.
The tender flowers o'ergrew the chasms deep,
    And God looked down, and saw that it was good.

ECCLESIASTES.

BECAUSE our life is but a little thing,
 Because the world is large, and we are small,
The misery of man is great on him,
 And one event still happeneth to all.

Of making many books there is no end,
 Much study still to weariness doth come;
But they who study not do brutish grow,—
 Man was not given language to be dumb.

Because there is that neither night nor day
 Gives sleep unto his eyelids, nor takes rest,
Some seeds of truth about the world do float,
 And here and there take root in some man's breast.

And as the flower, when it hath borne its fruit,
  Doth pass, we know not how, we know not
    where ;
So he who to the world hath given hope,
  Doth for his portion take the world's despair.

Because there cometh yet a darker time,
  Wherein the broken cisterns hold no more ;
Wherein the mourners go about the streets,
  And work, the last of joys, shall all be o'er ;—

Rejoice, O young man ! in thy pride of life,
  Sing, seer ! the songs that will not come again ;
But know that still for these the judgment waits,
  And God shall hold thee steward of thy pain.

"NAZARENE, THOU HAST CONQUERED!"

IN my haste I cried against Him,
  Faithful God and tender friend ;
I let fall the hand that held me,
  And I would myself defend.

Then for chastisement came scourging,
  When mine own hand held the rod,
And I found myself more cruel
  Than had ever seemed my God.

Deeper, deeper, sinking deeper,
  'Mid the thorns and in the mire ;
Still my heart held out against him,
  And my soul would not aspire.

I was angry with mine anguish,
   And I gnashed against my pain ;
And I stopped mine ears from hearing
   Pleading music, heavenly strain.

But a flash of tender sunshine
   Came and smote upon mine eyes ;
Then I swooned upon the pathway,
   And I dared not stir nor rise.

He of Nazareth had conquered,
   And I bathed me in His smile ;
Then He shewed a cord of crimson—
   He had held me, all the while.

PENITENCE.

BECAUSE I knew not when my life was good,
 And when there was a light upon my path,
But turned my soul perversely to the dark —
 O Lord, I do repent.

Because I held upon my selfish road,
And left my brother wounded by the way,
And called ambition duty, and pressed on—
 O Lord, I do repent.

Because I spent the strength Thou gavest me,
In struggle which Thou never didst ordain,
And have but dregs of life to offer Thee—
 O Lord, I do repent.

Because I chose the thorns and 'plained for flowers,
And pressed the sword-points down upon my heart,
And moaned that they did hurt me, like a child—
 O Lord, I do repent.

Because I struck at others in my pain,
Like some wild beast that, wounded, turns at bay,
And rends the innocent earth he stands upon—
O Lord, I do repent.

Because I was impatient, would not wait,
But thrust mine impious hand across Thy threads,
And marred the pattern drawn out for my life—
O Lord, I do repent.

Because I called good evil, evil good,
And thought I, ignorant, knew many things,
And deemed my weight of folly weight of wit—
O Lord, I do repent.

Because Thou hast borne with me all this while,
Hast smitten me with love until I weep,
Hast called me, as a mother calls her child—
O Lord, I do repent.

GOD'S WAY.

" For my thoughts are not your thoughts, saith the Lord."

I SAID, " The darkness shall content my soul ;"
  God said, " Let there be light."
I said, " The night shall see me reach my goal ;"
  Instead, came dawning bright.

I bared my head to meet the smiter's stroke ;
  There came sweet dropping oil.
I waited, trembling, but the voice that spoke,
  Said gently, " Cease thy toil."

I looked for evil, stern of face and pale ;
  Came good, too fair to tell.
I leant on God when other joys did fail ;
  He gave me these as well.

WITH GOD.

GOOD Lord, no strength I have, nor need ;
   Within Thy light I lie,
And grow like herb in sunny place,
   While outer storms go by.

Thy pleasant rain my soul doth feed—
   Thy love like summer rain ;
I faint, but lo thy winds of grace
   Revive my soul again.

I fain would give some perfume out,
   Some bruisèd scent of myrrh ;
But Thou art close at hand, my Lord—
   I need not strive nor stir.

I cannot fear, and need not doubt,
   Though I be weak and low :
If Thou didst will, a mighty sword
   From out my stem should grow.

Thou hast Thy glorious forest trees,
　　Thy things of worth and power;
But it may be Thy plan were marred
　　Had I ne'er lived a flower.

Thy promise, like an evening breeze,
　　Doth fold my leaves in sleep ;
Who trusts, the Lord will surely guard,
　　Who loves, the Lord will keep.

SOSPIRI VOLATE.

SOSPIRI VOLATE.

THUS I found them labelled,
 In an old bureau ;
Hands that wrote and eyes that read
 Withered long ago ;
Fulness of the story
 No one now can know.

Softly laid together
 All the letters now ;
Do they bend above them still,—
 Saints with radiant brow ?
" Gregory to Margaret."
 All is uttered now ;
Gone the seal of silence,
 That delayed their vow.

Should I burn them dumbly ?
 Half I thought it well.
'T was not mine, the sacred thing,
 Was it right to tell ?
Halo of its sacredness
 Should I thus dispel ?

Yet I thought an angel,
* Gone past all regret,*
Would be willing that its gems
* Should be roughly set ;*
If perchance some might from them
* Rays of brightness get.*

Life is strangely duplex :
* From the far-off past*
Come the things of yesterday,
* Shadows forward cast.*
'Tis the old old story,
* Earliest liveth last ;*
Lovers die, but love doth live—
* Darkness cometh fast.*

A PORTRAIT.

[Gregory.]

EYES like summer twilight grey,
   Tranquil as the sleeping sea ;
With a light from far away
   Shining softly all for me.

Hands that on the ruddy sands
   Gleam with whiteness, pale and fair,
With the gems of many lands
   Resting, strangely homelike, there.

Lips half-parted, where mine eyes
   Watch the words she will not speak ;
Watch the throbbing thoughts that rise
   With the flush that rounds her cheek.

Thus my lady sits at rest,
    While I dream beside her feet,
With the thought, all unexpressed,
    Sleep in Heaven were less sweet.

STRANGERS.

[Margaret.]

I DO not know your name, dear,
　　I do not know your rank,
And do not care for either ;
　　But heartily I thank
The chance, or fate, that made you
　　Go wandering that way,
The chance, or fate, that led you
　　To cross my path that day.

For I was drifting, drifting
　　Adown a grassy slope ;
A spell was laid upon me
　　With which I could not cope.
The air was faint with roses,
　　The sea lay like a mist,
The flowers beyond the sunlight
　　Were waiting to be kissed.

M

The waterfall kept dropping,
  " Drip, drip," for evermore ;
The little pool beneath it
  With diamonds ran o'er.
A word had just been spoken,
  The answer yet remained,—
A step upon the greensward,—
  I momently refrained.

Two stranger eyes bent on me,
  So grave, and pure, and sad,
Such eyes as those my brother,
  Who was not, might have had.
They changed my coming sentence
  From plausible to true :
I might have wrecked two lives, dear,
  If it had not been for you.

WALKING IN DARKNESS.

THE PURITAN POET.

[Gregory.]

THROUGH the wood where the serpent lies hidden asleep,
  If indeed he can sleep when a mortal is near ;
Up the way that is narrow, the path that is steep,
  With no guide for my footsteps, no help for my fear :
Only this—that He knoweth the way that I tread,
And His banner of crimson is over my head.

With the loneliness awful pressed into my soul,
  With no voice for companion, no grasp of a hand
With the dimmest of longings for dreamiest goal,
  With the reeds to support me, the oaks to withstand :
With this only for solace—God knoweth indeed
Where the poverty galls, of what things we have need.

With the traitor within me that whispers of rest,
　　Where the river flows swift, and the river flows deep ;
Where the nightshade hangs purple, with gold at its
　　　breast,
　　And the wild bees, awaking, would hum me to sleep :
Only this to withhold me—no sparrow can fall
But the angels are sorry, God knoweth it all.

With the thorns that seemed flowers pressed into my
　　feet,
　　With the herbs that are bitter, for wholesomest food;
While my lips shut in longing for poisonous sweet,
　　For the berries of scarlet that round me are strewed;
With the parching of thirst and impatient desire :
Only this to restrain me—"Still saved as by fire."

Can I kill half my nature, and leave half alive?
　　Keeping down all emotion, it burns me away.
Through the night I may toil, and in darkness may
　　strive,
　　But another must herald the dawning of day.
I have spent all my strength, and my journey is done :
Holy Father, receive me, through Jesus Thy Son.

QUIETNESS.

[Margaret.]

IS the world so very sad a place?
   Looking out here through geranium leaves,
We can see the sky all rosy grace,
   And can feel, what one of us believes,
That He giveth His belovèd sleep,—
Not in death alone we cease to weep.

Softly, shining cloudlets come and go,
   While the blue shows deeper in between,
And the very sunset leaves a glow
   Lovelier than all rays the day has seen :
Flecks of light make blossoms on the floor.
Silent music wraps us o'er and o'er.

Still and quiet, with intensest calm,
    As the centre of all motion rests ;
So we breathe away those hours of balm,
    Rise with strengthened hearts within our breasts.
Go, dear, but remember, through all weather,
We are friends—we were in Heaven together.

YOUTH AND MAIDENHOOD.

[Gregory.]

LIKE a drop of water is my heart
   Laid upon her soft and rosy palm,
Turned whichever way her hand doth turn,
   Trembling in an ecstasy of calm.

Like a broken rose-leaf is my heart,
   Held within her close and burning clasp,
Breathing only dying sweetness out,
   Withering beneath the fatal grasp.

Like a vapoury cloudlet is my heart
   Growing into beauty near the sun,
Gaining rainbow hues in her embrace,
   Melting into tears when it is done.

Like mine own dear harp is this my heart,
    Dumb, without the hand that sweeps its strings ;
Though the hand be careless or be cruel,
    When it comes, my heart breaks forth and sings.

FAITHFUL.

[Margaret.]

ONLY that, dear, neither wise nor fair,
  Just as commonplace as bread you eat,
Or as water flowing everywhere,
  Or the homely grass beneath your feet.
Only faithful,—does the want alarm you?
Only faithful,—will the word not charm you?

Faithful, as I read it, means just this—
  That henceforth I through the world shall go
Holy as an angel, by your kiss;
  Happy, though no other bliss I know.
Only faithful,—have you not repented?
Only faithful,—is your heart contented?

Faithful, dear, to keep or let you go,
 Faithful to give all and nothing take ;
Think you I should rave in angry woe,
 If by Time's fault you should me forsake ?
Only be yourself, though mine no longer ;
By your being I shall grow the stronger.

A SONG OF DRAGONS.

[*Gregory.*]

ALL-conquering dragons ! creep over the streets
   Which the city hath reared in the pride of her
      power ;
Beslime then with ruin, befoul them with heats,
  Let them lie in the dust as the things of an hour.

All-conquering dragons ! creep over the youths
   As they wrestle with Fate, and are vanquished and
      thrown ;
With hissing of facts and of palpable truths
  Let the burden of life to their souls be made known.

All-conquering dragons ! creep over the old ;
   Let them loosen the grasp that hath strengthened
      their days ;
Their wisdom die out, as a dream that is told,
  And the works of their life turn to frivolous plays.

All-conquering dragons! creep over the dead;
Let their honours fall from them, their memory die,
Unsceptred the hand, and uncrowned be the head,
In the waters of Lethe unwept let them lie.
Is it nothing to you, all ye men that pass by?

COMFORTING.

HOW shall I comfort thee, O friend of friends?
    If I were weeping, thou couldst comfort me
With just a touch upon my bowèd head ;
If I were blind, thy kiss should heal mine eyes,
And bring them into life and light again ;
If I were deaf, with sobs tempestuous
Thy voice would pierce the storm with " Peace, be
    still."
But thou, O friend, how can I comfort thee ?

With counsel ? but my wisdom is all thine,
The overflowings of thy bounteous spring ;
I have no knowledge, dear, but thou hast given,
No insight save what thou hast brought to me.

How can I guide? thou, only, know'st the way ;
I am but as the staff within thy hand—
A trusty staff,—lean on me, dear, I pray ;
But oh, my friend, how shall I comfort thee?

I can but weep with thee, O friend of friends,
And bid thee use me even as thou wilt.
Dost wish for smiles? they come at thy command :
For song? that, bird-like, only waits thy call.
Will dying serve thee? let me quickly die.
Will living serve thee? let me live for aye.
Such as my being is, 'tis wholly thine ;
But still, O friend, how shall I comfort thee?

PEASANT BARD TO NOBLE MISTRESS.

[**Gregory.**]

DO you think it, gentle lady, that because my name
is new,
I should bow before your lineage, should be humble,
dear, with you?
But I love you : do you hear it ? I have crowned you
with my crown;
And in Love's fair state, my lady, is no looking up nor
down.

Were you fifty times a princess, by your love I should
be king;
And our love would be the only thing that each of us
could bring.
Are you proud of ancient honours ?—I am prouder of
your grace.
Are you proud of famous kinsmen ?—I am prouder of
your face.

Do I shock your dainty hearing with these rugged
    rhymes of mine?—
'Tis the rugged tree, my lady, best supports the tender
    vine.
Were I shaft of polished granite, you have met such
    men before ;
Did they satisfy you, dearest? did you never crave for
    more?

With your regal state upon you, would you daunt me,
    O my queen?
But I stood you in the sunlight, and it made a brighter
    sheen.
Crimson robe might float about you ; but I only had to
    speak,
And the crimson, at my bidding, rose and beautified
    your cheek.

O mine empress! O my dearest! do you think me
    harshly. proud?
Would it please you, would not pain you, lead me out
    before the crowd ;
As a dog I lie beside you, on my neck your foot shall rest.
Ah, mine empress ! all indignant, doth she clasp me
    to her breast.

CITY MAID TO·COUNTRY LOVER.

[Margaret.]

THINK you, dear, that I could love you
　　Were you such a one as these—
Never looking up above you,
　　Never stirred by heavenly breeze ;
With their calm and courtly graces,
　　Deadly weak and false at heart,
With the smile upon their faces
　　Ghastly weary of its part ?

No, I will not wrong them, dearest,
　　Some are noble men and true ;
And I need not dim the clearest,
　　That he may look dull by you.
Such he must be, my one planet,
　　Bright with myriads, or alone,
As your Greek, howe'er you scan it,
　　Is the finest language known.

N

Think you, dear, that I go laughing
   All the busy day along,
Gaily wine of pleasure quaffing,
   Deep in picture or in song?
Know you not there is no pleasure   .
   But is holy on one side?
That I keep for you, my treasure,
   Share with you at eventide.

Know you not the garish real
   Never yet a maid enticed?
That a woman's one ideal
   Must be something like the Christ;
With the God-like, through the human,
   Shining crystalline and clear?
Would you really win a woman?
   Be her sanctuary, dear.

DOUBT.

[Gregory.]

HOW say they, dear, that doubt kills love?
  Such love doth need no killing;
The love that doubts is dead, my heart,
  Nor met its death unwilling.

Though all the world proclaim her false,
  Though night to morn should swear it;
No witnesses shall prove her fault,
  Till she herself declare it.

O doubting hearts! O callous hearts!
  Go through the world complaining.
Not love, but hate, is blind, O men;
  Ye lose by all your gaining.

A PLEA.

[𝔐argaret.]

TRUST me, dearest.   Could I ask it
   Did a shadow of untruth
Rear its ghostly front before me,
  Even from my vanished youth?
Were my life not crystal clear,
I would turn and leave you, dear.

Trust me, only for a little :
  I would trust you, dear, for aye,
With no plighted troth upon you,
  With your thoughts all free to stray.
Could your heart find fitter rest,
Mine should still keep empty nest.

Trust me, dearest, for your soul's sake :
   Could I be the thing you fear,
Then were love indeed a vileness,
   Better that it came not near.
Grapes from thistles men may glean,
Never stain from thing so clean.

GLORIANA.

[Gregory.]

WHERE the summer sun doth shine,
    On the green and fragrant vine,
There she dwelleth, maiden mine :
        Gloriana.

Not a learnèd lady she ;
Yet in truth her parts agree,
With a subtle harmony :
        Gloriana.

And the words so sweet, unwise,
To her rosy lips that rise,
Gain their power from her eyes :
        Gloriana.

We were young upon that day,
When we two did idly stray,
Laughing all the hours away :
    Gloriana.

We are young for evermore,
If you deign to share my store,
Store of love that runneth o'er :
    Gloriana.

CAPITULATION.

[Margaret.]

LOVE, do you love me, really and truly?
  If I submit to you, frankly and duly,
Will you, magnanimous, ease the surrender?
Will you be merciful, patient, and tender?
Will you, against myself, be my defender?

Love, if to-morrow word came I must leave you,
Would this, our happy time, cheer you or grieve you?
Would you then wish that you never had known me,
That I had left you in peacefulness lonely?
Would you be desperate, love, or sad only?

Love, only one thing is patent and certain,—
All of our past is shut off by a curtain,
Thick and impalpable as the night falling;
Never again shall the darkness enthralling
Hear us, like lonely birds, each to each calling.

Love, if but once had the sun, in his brightness,
Poured on the world all the flood of his whiteness,
Never again should the darkness unbroken
Reign as of old, ere the fiat was spoken ;
Day would have dawned, though but once.   Take the
    token.

GOOD-BYE.

[Gregory.]

GO, light of life, thou hast my heart's deep blessing,
   A whispered prayer, too fervent far to speak ;
Each sighing breeze shall be a mute caressing,
   An earnest of my love, so strong, so weak ;
So strong, that by its power my spirit trembleth
   At thine approach, within its inmost core ;
So weak, that nothing greater it resembleth
   Than little ripples heard in ocean's roar.
It cannot change the things which bid us sever,
   No matter at what cost of bleeding pain,
Which break the links that bound us so together,
   And bid us sail apart upon life's main.
Yet, better so than constantly to meet thee
   As light acquaintance, little loved or known,
To crush my heart that so it might not greet thee
   In hand to hand, or word, or look, or tone.

There is no need of any sigh or token
  That thou wilt not forget our olden love :
I am as sure of that which thou hast spoken
  As though it came on sunbeams from above.
Thine eyes must not be dim with tears, yet, dearest,
  Thy last look should be sunshine, breathe no sigh.
Thy head must rest once more where thou art
    nearest—
  Upon my heart, and then good-bye, good-bye.

THE REPLY.

[Margaret.]

I CANNOT speak, we grow so dumb with sorrow ;
  I cannot look, mine eyes are blind with tears ;
I cannot say, " We meet again to-morrow ; "
  I cannot gaze along the weary years.

" Good-bye, good-bye," the autumn air is sighing,
  The very flowers droop in sadness sweet,
Upon the hills a purple pall is lying,
  The stealthy waves creep up unto my feet.

O cruel waves! to bear away my gladness;
  O stedfast rock! to rest my hand upon;
O traitress heart! to melt away in sadness;
  O dazzling sunbeams! would ye never shone!

O little bloom of fragile faithful heather!
  Come, let me press my burning lips on you;
Come, teach me how to bear this stress of weather,
  And give my parchèd tongue a sense of dew.

Mine eyes, my poor wet eyes, are aching, aching;
  The heavy tears lie scorching on my cheek;
My heart is hungry, weary,—is it breaking?
  Good-bye, good-bye, I cannot, cannot speak.

SHELTERED.

[Margaret.]

M Y love, oh ! my love, in the darkness,
   While I have the warmth and light ;
Oh ! shine on him, stars out of heaven,
   And comfort him, Queen of Night.

My love, whom they called unbeliever,
   Because he had doubted them ;
My love, whom they called Pharisaic,
   Because he had dared condemn.

My love, in the ranks of the martyrs,
   No palm in his weary hand ;
So patiently walking in silence,
   For no one will understand.

My love, in his desolate greatness,
   Pursuing his stedfast way,
And thinking, perchance, in the twilight,
   Of words I was forced to say.

If bodily life were in danger,
   I then might hold out my hand ;
But as it is only his spirit,
   Our friendship must cancelled stand.

Oh, pitiful fashion of loving !
   Oh, pitiful pride of mine !
Love, come once again, I am waiting
   For thee, to be thine, all thine !

UNSHELTERED.

[Gregory.]

O ADAMANT regiment of houses !
   O commonplace walling me in !
O gates that but open on darkness !
   O thoroughfares leading to sin !

I fought, and I failed, and am vanquished !
   They will not be better for me ;
The people will go to destruction,
   The multitude will not be free.

Perhaps I mistook my vocation,
   Was " meant for a worker for bread,
And not for a Moses or Aaron "—
   'Twas wise, though 'twas sneeringly said.

One friend did believe in me truly,
   But that must have been a mistake,
As she must herself have discovered,
   Or else she would never forsake.

Well, others have suffered as I do ;
   I am but a sheep-dog grown old ;
Grown old in the spring of my manhood,
   I shrivel up here in the cold :

The cold, and the sleet, and the darkness,
   The oozing and fog-laden rain ;
Fit adjuncts of this, mine attainment,
   And meet for my bridal of pain.

A PRAYER OF BLESSING.

[Gregory.]

IN the day of thy sore distress,
  When the billows break over thee ;
When the greater woe drowns the less,—
  The Lord hear thee !

In the time of thy famine and night,
  When thy trouble shall weary thee ;
When the darkness shall conquer the light,—
  The Lord hear thee !

When the bow in thy hands shall hang faint,
  And the archers encompass thee ;
When thy weakness shall utter its plaint,—
  The Lord hear thee !

When thy life, with its love and its strife,
  Like a garment shall fall from thee ;
When thy soul shall wait at the crystal gate,—
  The Lord hear thee !

WAITING.

[Margaret.]

DID you call me, O my lover, did you call me?
　　Was it you that sent a thrill across the dark?
Come in any shape, O love, 'twill not appal me,
Voice or presence, ghost or music, dear, I hark.

Are you living, O my lover, are you mortal?
Is there flesh upon the hand stretched out to mine?
Man's or angel's, it shall draw me past the portal
In the distance, where the sprinkled lintels shine,
Shewing forth, in crimson drops from the Atonement,
That, from henceforth, love and sorrow are divine.

———

　　If he would come but once again,
　　　　Oh I would kneel so lowly!
　　My lips should drain his wound of pain,
　　　　And satisfy him wholly.

I wonder if one died of joy
    How long would be the dying?
'Twere better so than bliss should cloy,
    And smiling turn to sighing.

I could not tire, though endless years
    Should stretch their weight above me ;
But other whither reach my fears,
    If he should cease to love me !

Ah love, dear love ! before that day,
    Destroy me, dear, I pray thee ;
Let Love's last kiss kiss life away,
    And Love, in dying, slay me.

GREETING.

[**Gregory.**]

L IFE of my life, light of my days,
How shall I sing thee, how utter thy praise?
Soft little hand, leading me still,
Spirit of Heaven, that guards me from ill.
Life of my life, light of my days,
I can but love thee, 'tis seraphs should praise.

Soul of my soul, shining on high,
I, looking earthwards, should falter and die,
Did not her love lighten my feet,
Did she not shine on me, calm and so sweet.
Soul of my soul, tender and wise,
Others may sing thee, I live in thine eyes.

Music of life, all it can know,
Though we be parted like viol from bow,
Still on the winds harmonies float,
Still our souls' converse comes, note for note.
Music of life, solemn and low,
Follow my footsteps, wherever they go.

AFAR OFF.

[Margaret.]

EYES that once looked into mine,
    Changing, softening, shining ;
Hair that round my heart did twine
    As we two, reclining,
Wooed the sweet from heather spray,
Lived our love one summer day ;—
Does it live yet, far away ?
    Am I, only, pining ?

Pining, said I ?—not for me
    Be the joyous being,
Satisfied to wander free,
    Satisfied with seeing.
Where my lover once hath trod,
Ever sacred be the sod,
Dedicate, as if to God,
    Till he will its freeing.

Vanished as a fallen tear,
 Sight and sound endearing ;
Silence, darkness, linger here,—
 Think you I am fearing ?
Fear for men of feeble mould,
Fear for maids whose hearts are cold ;—
Thus shall be our story told,
 Sweet will be the hearing.

SYMPHONY.

[Gregory.]

IF I were drowned in darkness
   While she did float in light,
Then I could dream the hours away,
  Nor dread the coming night.

If I alone kept fealty
  And she did lightly stray,
Then I should know she ne'er had been,
  And turn my thoughts away.

If only for her loving
  I loved this maiden mine,
It might be that my soul would seek
  Some nearer clinging vine.

If she had ever a sister,
   If I had ever a brother,—
But in all the world we have no mate,
   We two, but just each other.

FAULT-FINDING.

[Margaret.]

SOME one said,
He is no friend who will not tell my faults.
And so I sat me down to look for thine,
To mark the sable flaws that fleck thine ermine.

I found a scorn unwise for things ignoble,
A power of silent wrath consuming wrong,
A way of digging deep below the sunshine,
A doubt of self, and trust in other men ;
I said, " These are thy follies."

I found a habit of self-sacrifice,
A tardy vision of rights personal,
A way of stepping back from thrusting crowds,
A loose light hold of things material ;
I said, " There thou art wrong."

I found,—but lo ! the thorns are blossoming !
It is a sacred rod my hand hath touched ;
Who counts the petals of a passion-flower ?
I know thy faults, dear, and they are thy crown.

A DREAM.

[Gregory.]

L OVE, I was dreaming, was dreaming,
　　It is better to sleep than to wake,
You and I were at rest, in the land of the blest,
　　You had followed me there for love's sake.

We were standing, like children, a-gazing
　　On the Lamb, and His white white throne ;
We were listening mute to the sound of the lute,
　　For the song was a song unknown.

And a shadow came over our spirit,
　　As we opened our mouths and were dumb ;
There was light in the air, there was melody there,
　　But no angel to us said " Come."

There were glittering mansions around us,
    Which we fain would have claimed for our own ;
But on each was a name, writ in letters of flame,
    And the name was a name unknown.

Then we sorrowful grew, being strangers,
    And you looked in my face, and you said,
" Is this Heaven indeed ? but I still am in need.
    Is this life ? then I fain were dead."

We went wandering, wandering, wandering,
    Far away from the shining throne ;
For on all who stood there was a garment so fair,
    And the garb was a garb unknown.

Then one came to us, radiant with greeting,
    But he spoke with a tongue unknown,
And we saw that his lips had been touched as with fire,
    And his brow with a white white stone.

Then he led us away to the portal,
    Led us out by the pearly gate ;
With a wave of the hand he commanded to stand
    Where he left us, to stand, and wait.

It was terrible there in the darkness,
  But we dared not complain nor moan,
For the silence of Heaven enthralled us in peace,
  And we waited for things unknown.

Then One came with a countenance wondrous,
  With the mark of a wound in His side;
And we fell at His feet in an ecstasy sweet,
  For we knew Him for one that had died.

" Little children," He said, "little children,
  Is it well that ye entered alone,
With no angel to guide you, no spirit beside you,
  With your coming unwatched for, unknown?"

Then we fell at His feet, in an agony sweet,
  And we wept in a passion of shame;
" We were weary, O Lord, we were pierced with thy
    sword, —
  On the wings of our longing we came."

Then He shewed us a mansion unfinished,
  With our name on the topmost stone;
And He said, "It doth wait till your souls are full grown;
  Ye reap not until ye have sown.

" Know ye not that your life is no discord ?
    There is never a note to spare ;
There is never a sigh ye can breathe till ye die
    But it maketh the harmony there.

" Life is one, all along, little children,
    From the first to the last it is known ;
There are tears shed on earth that are seeds sown for
        Heaven,—
    Ye reap not until ye have sown."

Then He led us away through the shadows,
    And we took up our burden of pain ;
But He said, " Lo, I go with you always, mine own ;
    Ye must never be vanquished again."

As our eyes gained their vision He vanished,
    But we felt that we were not alone ;
As He rose we could hear, through the dark sounding
        clear,—
    " Ye reap not until ye have sown."

Love, I was dreaming, was dreaming,
    It is better to sleep than to wake ;
You and I were at rest, in the land of the blest,
    You had followed me there for love's sake.

MOUNTAIN PASSES.

[Margaret.]

COURAGE, dear heart, we must not both despair :
   Somewhere the sun is shining, even now—
Shining on laughing brooks and meadows fair,
   Stirring the very breeze that frets your brow.
Surely the path will open farther on,
'Tis but a little way that we have gone.

Yes, it is hard—the drenching blinding mist
   That, if it could, would shut me out from you ;
The snake Despair that from its fastness hissed ;
   The fair false Hope that to the ravine drew ;
But we were saved, we are God's children yet,
He will not let us go, though we forget.

Even on this our toilsome way there come
  Sweet scents from bruisèd flowers, and winds astray ;
The sound of sunshine in the wild bees' hum ;
  While, tamed with fear, the birds around us play.
The very dumb things gain some good from harm,—
Courage from fright, and boldness from alarm.

Still it is hard—no darkness will be light,
  Though we should call it light from night till morn ;
We can but wait until the dawning bright
  Shall shew us how it was we were forlorn ;
Not all forlorn,—through deepest darkness, friend,
Love's joy alone doth never change nor end.

MEETING.

[Gregory.]

ONLY a look that questioned me, " True, still ?"
    Only mine eyes that answered back, " True,
      still."
If I had faltered once, had swerved but once,
If I had wandered, dreaming, past our faith,
Then the soft eyes had slain me, left me dead.

Only this faith of ours between us, love ;
Only this anchor, buried in deep seas :
Two ships that sail apart all round the world,
Yet hold together in the quiet deep,—
Calm overhead, or storm, the anchor holds.

Solemn as death in life this faith of ours ;
Dear as the last faint smile in dying eyes ;
Holy as little children, bright as morn ;
Fair as the first red dawn in summer skies,
Strong with the strength that withers not nor dies.

RITORNELLO.

[Margaret.]

I KNEW your soul would come, my love,
  To comfort mine in pain ;
But I did not dream to see your face,
  Nor hear your voice again :
I only knelt to God and said,
  " From prayer I refrain."

I dare not keep you here, my love ;
  My knight must hold his place,—
With the noblest in the land must ride,
  And foremost in the race.
'Tis his diviner self I love,
  The strength that tempers grace.

Yet stoop from off your horse, my love,
    And kiss me on my cheek ;
Let my head be lifted high, my love,
    'Tis still beneath you meek.
Ride out, ere tears shall blind me, love ;
    Good-bye, while I can speak.

ADRIFT.

[**Gregory.**]

STRONG, did you think me, my darling?
  Yes, I was strong with you;
Man, with a woman's deep heart in his hand,
  Unto no king need sue.
And I thought, in the pride of my manhood,
  I could know you alive in the world,
And rejoice in the joy of your being,
  Though I might from your daïs be hurled.

But I cannot, my darling, my darling!
  You must die from me; perish, O sweet;
Let your music be silent, my bird, my bird!
  I must listen no more for your feet.
Let your visage be veiled, O mine angel,
  I am dazzled and burnt in its light;
Let me out to my compeers, like Judas,
  Let me out to the desolate night.

Welcome foes, be ye human or demon,
    Strike me now while my bosom is bare ;
There is never a thrust that shall wound me,
    There is nothing can injure despair.
Beat on me, whirlwinds from Heaven,
    Hiss at me, fiends below ;
Girt with the girdle of him who has naught,
    Out on my way I go.

NEVER AGAIN.

[**Margaret.**]

NEVER again to touch my hand in greeting,
  Never again to lay your lips on mine.
Was it in Paradise joy grew so fleeting?
  Was the world old when Eve did all resign?
Poor resignation, gone past all retaining,
Poor resignation, gone past all regaining.

Never again to know I need but live,
  Just be myself, and one would count it blessing;
Carelessly, as the birds their carols give,
  Joyously, as a child receives caressing.
Never again the bliss of gladness giving,
Never again the life of perfect living.

Never again; between us lies all Heaven,
  Only by God's great hand I reach you, friend;
All other ways are marred with evil leaven,
  All other ways to ill and sorrow tend.
Never again, thou shalt not hear my weeping,
Never again,—Christ hold thee in his keeping!

TRYSTING TIME.

[Gregory.]

MARGARET, hear me !
  Come once again.
Is all forgotten ?
  Love drowned in pain ?

Did we not promise,
  Back in the past,
That we would meet, love,
  Once at the last ?

That, with Death's benison
  Joining our hands,
One should be left at sea,
  One on the sands.

Dim is the sea, love,
  Fog on the shore,
Only your promise,
  Ask I no more.

Margaret, Margaret!
  How can I die
Till you have wished me
  Once more, Good-bye!

IN THE POLAR SEAS.

[𝕸𝖆𝖗𝖌𝖆𝖗𝖊𝖙.]

YES, I had lost thee, for one day, one life,—
   The days get blurred where never shines the
      sun ;
My hand had dropped from thine, and I was tired,
  Longing for death ere life had well begun.
I laid me down beside the green grey sea,
And never dreamt that thou wouldst seek for me.

Mine was the loss, the loneliness, the need ;
  Thine was the strength, the vision, and the speech.
The floating ice came nearer, nearer yet,—
  There was no help that my weak hand could reach.
I laid me down beside the green grey sea :
It never said that thou wouldst seek for me.

Deeper and deeper struck the deadly cold,
   Even my love was wrapped in snowy sleep ;
My hand had ceased to grope for thine ; mine eyes,
   Frozen to blankness, would not stir nor weep.
I laid me down beside the green grey sea,
And said " 'Tis well ; he will not seek for me."

The time went on,—I think a thousand years,
   For I was old, and young again, and old,—
Until a sudden glory struck the skies,
   Above the horizon shone a globe of gold :
The sun has risen o'er the crimson sea—
O love ! is't true, hast come to seek for me?

DEAD MY LOVE IS DEAD.

[Margaret.]

THE pure, grave eyes will never smile again,
 Will never change in love, or joy, or pain;
The tender mouth is closely folded now,
The quiet hair lies lightly on his brow.
He used to toss it back—the wavy hair,
And I would envy it for lying there,
And press my yearning fingers there instead,—
And now, my love is dead, my love is dead!

How strange it feels—the very scent of flowers
Is just the same as when we called them ours;
The little rose-bud pressed into his hand
Fades not so soon as when he used to stand
And say that I should have it for a kiss,
And watch my longing ripen into bliss,
The while he stooped to me his kingly head,—
And now, my love is dead, my love is dead!

I wonder when he died—was't yesternight ?
It seems a lifetime since I saw the light ;
I live in twilight now—a soft, sweet calm
That stills my weeping, like a breath of balm ;
It seems as though his very presence here
Distilled the burning out of every tear.
I never thought I could have lived and said,
" My love is dead, my love is dead, is dead ! "

AFTER.

[𝕸𝖆𝖗𝖌𝖆𝖗𝖊𝖙.]

WAIT for a moment, Death, I pray you wait;
    I have been waiting years, O friend, for you.
Now that your hand holds mine in firmest grasp,
Let me look back, ay, even from Heaven, to view
All the dear earth, and make my last adieu.

Mountains and purple mists and valleys green,
Rivers and moaning seas and lakes asleep,
Little white houses where the people live,
One little house where mourners watching keep,—
No, I am still, good Death; souls cannot weep.

Yet it is fair, the earth, so fair, so good!
Suffer me, O ye friends who dwell therein,
While I implore you not to spurn the earth;
Surely to slight God's work is bitter sin,
Surely God does not end where men begin.

Must it be so then, Death,— my tale half told?
Must I then leave my message incomplete?
All that I would have said will some one say—
Some one with wings where I had weary feet?
Let it be so,—one day we all shall meet.

NATURE APOSTATE.

SONG OF THE WATER-NIXIES.

BY the ripple, ripple of the shallow sea,
        By the rocky sea,
        By the hollow sea,
We have built a giant windmill, with its long arms free,
        And it grinds, that we
        May not hungry be.
With a rumble and a roar, sounding all along the
    shore,
We should vanish and should perish if our wheel
    were heard no more.

Little hopes of fisher maidens in the far-off town,
        In our wheel go down,
        Evermore go down,
For the fisher lads that hold them in the deep sea
    drown ;
        By our grinding drown,
        For our pleasures drown.

Rend the garment from the soul ; let it go, we care not
    where ;
What do mortals want with spirit ? 'tis the bodies
    that are fair.

Out beyond the green horizon lurks the vengeful
    day,
            Lurks the fateful day,
            Lurks the hateful day,
When the winds shall cease to help us in our shark-
    like play,
            When our calm cold sway
            Shall have passed away,
When the wreckers and the wrecked both at peace
    shall be,—
When the threat shall be fulfilled, and there be no
    more sea.

THE WAR-CRY OF THE WINDS.

DASHING against the mountain,
   Crashing along the hill ;
Hurrah for the mighty storm-blast !
   Man lies still :

Blind with the dazzling lightning,
   Deaf with the thunder roar,
His boast as the lord of nature
   Heard no more.

Cowering like the tyrant
   Hurled from his paper throne ;
The king of the whole creation
   Maketh moan.

Batter him, winds, and beat him,
   Scatter his ships at sea ;
We owe him a debt of arrogance,—
   Winds are free.

What though we turn his windmills,
What though we grind his corn?
The mill, and the man, and the grinding,
Cease at morn.

He to be end of all things!
Never to pass away!
When the last of the men has perished,
Winds shall play.

SNOWDON TO VESUVIUS.

BROTHER, across the sea I send you greeting,
  I, standing here in calm that is not peace,
Bound to respect these pigmies at my feet,
Do envy you the power to maim and slay,
To thrust aside these fretting human things
That call themselves our masters, and are vile.
Was ever yet a stone that told a lie?
A rock that did betray his nearest friend?
A stream that smiled towards the loathsome dark?
A wind that turned itself i' the hand of God,
And smote where He was blessing?   Thus do men.

VESUVIUS.

'Tis true, the race is feeble, strangely weak,
Shifting as stormy breezes, varying oft,
And worn to death with just a moment's life.
But all frail things have some peculiar strength,
And man is strong in loving.

                              I have heard
That on this ground he even can meet God,
And stand before Him, interchanging thought
As with an equal.
                    Once on Mount Moriah
The very meekest, gentlest of them all,
Stood thus with God until he kindled so,
His visage was all burning, unconsumed.
And once, upon the Mount of Calvary,
'Twas said the Son of God Himself came down
For love of man, and suffered many things,
Even the pang called death.

                    SNOWDON.

Strange! that a race with such capacities
Should sink so low! 'Tis true the mountain's height
Doth make the valley's depth; but never yet
Was known a mountain that refused to rise;
That, ass-like, supine, did resist the good,
And plant itself dead level.
                              But these men
They use not even this, their power of love;

And, after all these centuries of light,
Have still no rule of right for questions vext,
Save springing at each other's throats like dogs.
Nay, I have known them meaner than the dogs,
Snarling and snarling, daring not to fight—
Whole nations, in their puny arrogance,
Vomiting evil words across the seas,
Until the air grew sulphurous with spite,
And cannon came to clear it.

VESUVIUS.

                              Yet I saw,
Only the last time when mine inward fires
Did grow too strong upon me and burst forth,—
I saw a youth, a careless, laughing youth,
Who, hearing moans for help beneath the wreck,
Did fling himself upon the scorching ash,
And dig and dig, with feet and fingers charred,
All quick with pain acute, dug on and on,
Until he rescued thence a stranger lad,
Of whom he knew just this,—that he was man,
And man in need.

And I have faith in man,
That some time, surely, he will wake to feel
His brotherhood, deep underlying all,
The kinship that is given him for strength,
The strange, mysterious soul which he alone
Doth hold in common only with his kind.
And if it be so, if the time should come
When men shall all be one, as once 'twas said
They were one man, then, as in those fair days,
The earth shall be subdued, and all our powers,
No more rebellious, shall before him bow,
The worthy subjects of a worthy King.

BY COMMAND.

M Y king sat out on his castle wall,
  And a royal command gave he :
" Come hither, come hither, ye people all,
  And a fairy tale bring me,
For of grammar, and crammer, and orthodox hammer,
  I have had quite enough," quoth he.

My liege's kingdom is small as yet,
  And his subjects are only two ;
And sometimes it happens his Grace will fret,
  "Why, you dear, I have only you !"
And in such sad case it becomes my place
  The imperial will to do.

So I peeled a willow, so white, so white,
   The wand that the fairies love ;
And I gathered the meadow-sweet, soft and light,
   And the fox's crimson glove ;
And I made a couch for the first stray sprite,
   With the down of a silver dove.

      Fairy, come home !
      Fairy, come home !
   Where hast thou wandered to ?
      Where dost thou roam ?
      Here is thy dwelling,
        Here is thy place ;
     Fairy king, fairy king,
       Show us thy face !

Three times round the meadow
   The little song did go ;
Then there came a peal of bells
   Chiming soft and low :

" Coming, coming, coming ;
   No one need to wait,
Wearily beseeching,
   At the fairy gate.

" For the fairies, like the mortals,
   Love to be loved ;
And the fairy palace portals
   Lightly are moved."

Then a rain of footsteps
   Sounded on the sward,
And a page came kneeling—
   " What wills my lord ? "

" I will a tournament," said he,
   " Where no one shall be killed ;
Where all shall gain the victory,
   And be supremely skilled."

Up rode a fairy paladin,
   With coat of beetle's mail ;
Before the glistening green and gold
   Sure any heart must quail.

" I see no foe," the king complained.
   " But wait," the page implored.
And then the fairy paladin
   Drew out a shining sword ;

R

He cut and thrust all round about,
   At neither sight nor sound,
Until a dastard knight they saw
   Lie dead upon the ground.

" The pledge is broken ! " cried the king.
   " Not so," the knight replied ;
" It was my meaner self I slew,—
   I live, though it has died."

Again the paladin rode forth,
   And this time seemed to seek
Some traitor that eluded him—
   The little king must speak :
" Where is the foe, Sir knight, on whom
   You would your vengeance wreak ? "

" It was a falsehood," said the knight,
   " They uttered of my friend ;
I tracked it down, and hunted it,
   And thus its life doth end ! "

Once more the paladin rode forth—
   Beneath his horse's feet
There seemed to be an enemy

That he was loth to meet ;
" Can you fear anything, Sir knight ? "
His smile was sad and sweet.

" It was a cruel injury,
An unforgiven pain ;
But there it lieth tranquilly,—
It will not stir again."

Then lightly springs my little king,
And merrily he sings,
" I too will be a paladin,
And fight with evil things."

FLOWERS IN THE EAST WIND.

PITIFUL, tender, sweet,
    With the dumb, bound woe,
With the stems that stoop, and the leaves that droop—
    Why should they suffer so ?

Bitterness hasteth, fleet,
    'Tis the south wind waits ;
While the fragrance dies, and the dead bud lies
    Close at our garden gates.

Oh, for a little space
    Where a child might tread,
Where a flower might grow into beauty, so
    Crowning the storm-bent head.

How can you tell what grace
    With a young thing dies?
What the world may lose while the doctors choose
    Which way the danger lies?

Slowly, with heavy feet,
    Do the great ones go;
While they try the right, and obey dull might,
    Doing not what they know.

Pitiful, human, sweet,
    Oh little children's eyes!
With the marks of weeping, and lack of sleeping—
    Woe for us when ye rise.

CHILD-LOVE.

L ITTLE eyes so softly wooing,
     Purely blind and purely wise ;
Knowing naught of evil-doing,
     Knowing much of good, dear eyes :
Shining on me, holy, sweet,
Gentle thoughts your gaze should meet.

Little hands with restless motion
     Fluttering about my cheek ;
Little feet with swift commotion
     Rushing some new joy to seek :
Bringing tidings fearlessly,
Never doubting sympathy.

Little heart so swiftly gladdened,
     Little soul so soon cast down ;
Little lips with curves so saddened
     By a moment's passing frown.
Let me humbly kneel beside thee,
Only God is fit to guide thee.

MIRIAM'S LULLABY.

IN a bed of rushes woven,
   Sleep, my baby, sleep.
Gurgling water lapping round him,
   Watch and ward to keep;
While the reeds spread out above him
   Shadows still and deep.

River, river, flowing past him,
   Bear his tears away;
River, river, flowing to him,
   Bring him joy, I pray;
Softest breezes, lily-scented,
   Round his beauty play;
Hush thee, dearest, fairest, rarest,
   Here I must not stay.

Clinging hands must loose me, loose me,
   Kissing lips be dry;
Longing eyes grow dim and dreamy,
   Curls in quiet lie.
Baby must in peace forget me,
   And his love must die;
Hush thee, dear, though I be weeping,
   Soon our days go by.

ROY'S PLAINT.

IT is so cold in all the world, with mother lying dead;
    I only want to go to sleep, but we must rouse, they
      said.
I wonder why they harass us, and will not let us lie;
The door is wide, and we will hide, my little Fan and I.

Yes, just a dog, and nothing more; but I have naught
    beside,
And mother's hand was laid on her the moment that
    she died;
And they loved one another so—where's mother,
    little Fan?
Ay, raise your head and whine, my dog, and call her
    if you can.

So patiently she bears with me the gnawing hunger-
    pain,
The bitter cold, and choking fog, and heavy blinding
    rain ;
I wish the stars would shine out once, before another
    day,—
There are no stars, so father said, in Heaven far away.

Cling closer, closer, little Fan, and let me feel you near;
I cannot see nor hear you now—I'm growing stupid,
    dear ;
And yet just now there seemed to come an awful flash
    of light :
I wish you had gone first, my dog !—my little Fan,
    Good-night !

MARJORY'S WEDDING.

MARJORY made her a wedding feast,
   "And I am to be the bride," said she.
"Wait for the bridegroom," was whispered then ;
  "What does that matter?" said Marjorie.

Marjory gathered the peaches fine,
   That dropped in the sun behind the tree.
"Where is your husband to share the feast?"
  "I can eat peaches," said Marjorie.

Feasting makes fractious, and some one said,
  "The wives that are beaten, better be."
Marjory kissed at the mirror's face ;
  "There is my beating," said Marjorie.

" If you were pretty, would you be good?"
So somebody said to Marjory.
" I cannot tell," said the maiden wild;
" Plenty of people are good, you see."

Softly the sunset crept over the hill,
Soft, like a shadow-land, glistened the sea;
Two little hands 'neath a head bent down:
" I am so tired!" said Marjorie.

POESY AND THE POET.

THE fairy queen Cophetua
   Went out one summer day;
She saw a little beggar lad
   Asleep upon the way.

His feet were torn with many thorns,
   His hands like dead hands lay,
And here and there across his cheek
   A drowsy tear did stray.

The fairy queen Cophetua,
   She knelt beside his head,
And raised it on her royal lap
   As on a mossy bed.

She felt a breath of deep repose
   Steal through his troubled sleep;
And then the queen Cophetua
   Did softly 'plain and weep :

"Oh this my king for whom I wait,
   Why need he suffer so?
Does no one know his coming state?
   His rank does no one know?

" I tell you, all ye elements,
   That he shall rule one day;
How dare ye buffet him full sore
   With your unruly play?"

Thereon the Wisdom King arose,
   The lord of all the fays:
" O daughter, anger is not truth,
   Nor adulation praise.

" Didst thou not scorn the fairy knights
   As gossamer and vain?
The fay who toys with human love
   Must wed with human pain."

" I will not," said the fairy queen;
   " I hate this thing called pain."
But softly sighed the sleeping lad,
   And down she knelt again.

His heavy-lidded eyes awoke,
   He gazed into her face.
"O queen of all my wanderings,
   Wilt grant me this one grace?

"If I should conquer, let it be
   By holy love of thee;
If I be vanquished, let me die
   Where I thy face can see."

Then lowly, lowly stooped the queen,
   And softly kissed his cheek.
Thereon the Wisdom King arose,
   And solemnly did speak:

"Go, mortal, on thy toilsome quest,
   Not pain but doubt is o'er;
The knight who once the queen has kissed
   Is hers for evermore."

WANDERING WILLIE.

WILLIE went out one morning
  The rising sun to see ;
He heard a rivulet laughing,
  "I follow you home," said he.
The river had run for a thousand years,
  Willie had lived for three.

Down by the singing river
  The rushes made their bed ;
"I am the king of the castle,"
  Said Will, with haughty head ;
He shouldered a reed for a musket,
  And went with martial tread.

Old Mother Sheep was feeding :
  "What brings that boy this way ?"
Slowly she followed Willie,
  And Willie edged away ;
One of the two was in earnest,
  Neither enjoyed the play.

"This is the giant," said Willie,
  "And I am the valiant knight;
If only he would not come quite so close,
  I think I should like to fight."
But the sheep came closer, and closer yet,
  And Willie grew white with fright.

Over the hedge went Willie,
  And into the ditch fell he,
But the ground was dry, and nothing was hurt,
  Only one dimpled knee.
"This is the mortal combat,
  And I am the slain," said he.

"Carry me home, ye maidens,"
  As nurse with a frown appears.
"I am a weary pilgrim,
  Lost for a hundred years."
"Minutes," said nurse, serenely—
  She may have had private fears.
"Did you not miss me?" said Willie;
  The hero dissolved in tears.

CRUTCH, THE JUDGE.

PATTER, patter, on the floor,
  Such a floor for hobbling,
In and out the open door,
  Where his sire sits cobbling :

Mat the merry, Mat the wise,
  So the children call him ;
Mat, with solemn, sightless eyes—
  Nought but good befal him !

Mat the cripple, poor and young,
  Lord of all his alley ;
Ruling by his gentle tongue,
  Bright with many a sally.

Mat and I fell out one day
  On a point of duty ;
I maintaining life was gay,
  And that truth was beauty,

I forgot, as he forgot,
    All his woe and blindness;
No one heard how hard his lot,
    Save as bringing kindness.

Now he only bowed his head
    O'er the crutch beside him,
While with gentle mirth he said,
    "Crutch, the Judge, has tried him.

"Crutch, the Judge, most learned stick,
    Sentenced that free lancer."
"Sentenced whom?" I questioned, quick;
    "Mat, the fool," came answer.

"Mat, who planned his life before,
    As a rush to glory,
Now, contented, lame, and poor,
    Only dreams his story."

"Tell me all the dream," I prayed,
    Creeping nearer, nearer;
For his face, in sorrow's shade,
    Shone with beauty clearer.

S 2

" All my dream I may not tell,
　No one now may share it ;
Yet in truth it pleased me well,
　Certain scars declare it."

Then I saw, how, while he smiled,
　There were marks of weeping
Held their place all unbeguiled :
　Nearer I came creeping.

" Tell me, Mat."　" I may not tell—
　There is might in duty :
Only know, one may live well
　Void of joy and beauty.

" If an angel came to-night
　Proffering all Heaven,
For this life, so bare of light,
　Bringing lustres seven,

" I would put the gift away
　With becoming meekness ;
I would rather live my day—
　There is strength in weakness."

Thus he spake—I could but hark :
　Like an organ pealing,
Pealing softly through the dark,
　Spake he, wounding, healing.

But the angel came that night,
　Tempted him too strongly ;
Mat escaped to boundless light,
　Crutch, the Judge, judged wrongly.

Mat, the cripple, was not meant
　Lame to go for ever :
Life's great law is discontent—
　None that knot may sever.

SERVANT AND MASTER.

I HAD a page, a little page,
  Who served me all the day,
Whose lute did sing my joyfulness,
  And charm my griefs away.

I decked him with my riband blue,
  And called him all mine own,
And thought with pride, " It will be good
  When this my page is grown."

I had a knight, a dainty knight,
  Who oftentimes rebelled,
And many a struggle sharp had we
  Whose pride should first be quelled ;

And sometimes he, and sometimes I,
   Would guide the tell-tale strain;
He troubled me full-sore, but oh,
   Would he were back again!

I have a king, a doughty king,
   Who rules me night and day;
And where he will he carries me,
   And will not let me stray.

No hidden treasure may I keep,
   No gaping wound conceal;
"Noblesse oblige," is all his creed;
   " Thy tears may some one heal."

LAMENTS.

ESAU.

ALL the day long have I laboured, my Father, my
    Father,
Sent by thy word from thy presence to serve afar off;
Now it is ended, and all is as dead leaves before thee;
Waste is my toil, and my hope, and my joy and reward.
Only my bitterness have I to bring thee, my Father;
Yet, for my needs' sake, I pray thee, bless me, even
    me.

Rugged and heavy of speech am I, Father, my Father:
E'en for another I could not plead smoothly and well;
And for myself I am dumb, O my Father, my Father,
Dumb as a beast that is smitten and can but be still.
Yet hast thou known me and loved me of old, O my
    Father,
Now, for thy love's sake, I pray thee, bless me, even
    me.

Haste thee to bless me, my Father, for swiftly there
    cometh
That which to us is the night, though to thee 'tis the
    dawn.
How can I suffer my life with no blessing upon it?
Where should I turn for a blessing, but only to thee?
Thou art my light, O my Father, all else is as darkness;
Now, for my woe's sake, I pray thee, bless me, even
    me.

ANDROMACHE.

A TOUCH upon my shoulder, a kiss upon my hair,
    And then the world was empty, and darkness
        everywhere,
Except where in the dimness, a ruby-eyed Despair
Sat glaring, glaring at me, and calling from her lair :
    " Andromache, Andromache."

The evil gods will follow where Hector heads the fray,
It irks them that a mortal should nobler be than they;
I see their airy weapons, already poised to slay,
I hear their backward whispers, as tauntingly they say:
    " Andromache, Andromache."

How say you that my grief is shared with Hector's sire
    and son ?
The babe has only smiles for life, his woes are not
    begun ;
And Priam, well he knows for him all suffering is
    done,
Ere long he will contented call on me, his only one :
      " Andromache, Andromache."

The pain is mine, as he is mine, my Hector, king and
    lord ;
For me alone he keeps his love, for all the world his
    sword ;
'Twill be my name that from his lips shall be with life
    outpoured,
Though neither gods nor men may hear the tender
    dying word :
      " Andromache, Andromache."

JERUSALEM.

O CITY of delight !
If thou hadst known, even thou, in that day,
Thou hadst not turned away,
In blind and angry spite,
When He whose love did shadow thee,
Like shadow of the cedar tree,
Watched by thee day and night.

O city desolate!
If thou hadst known, in that time of pride,
The shame thou couldst not hide,
That festered in thy gate,
When He, the King unrecognized,
Did come unknown, and pass unprized,
And pitifully wait.

O city overthrown !
If thou hadst known, ah me ! if thou hadst known,
Thou hadst not been as stone
When love that died did moan ;
Thy time of fructifying rain
Had not gone out in barren pain.—
Thy harvest will not come again,
Now thou art left alone.

QUEEN ELIZABETH.

DYING, and loth to die, and longed to die ;
    Is there no pity, O my land, my land?
Is it as naught to you, ye passers-by ?
    Will ye not, for a moment, listening stand ?

Who shall come after me, is what ye pray;
    Truly ye have not spared me all my days.
Tudor, the grand old race, may pass away :
    Stuart the weak and false, awaits your praise.

Essex, my murdered darling, tender one,
    Should have been here, my people, but for you;
Now he but haunts me,—oh my son, my son !
    Would that the queen had erred, the friend been true

T

Dudley, my one one love, my spirit halts;
  Would that it had thine now on which to lean;
Faulty thou wert, they said; come back, dear faults,—
  Have I not right to pardon, as a queen?

Truly, 'tis hard to rule, 'tis sore to love,
  All my life long the two have torn my heart;
Now that the end has come, all things to prove,
  I but repent me of my chosen part.

Now to my mother's God, who dwells afar,
  Come I, a broken queen, a woman old;
Smirched with the miry way my soul hath trod,
  Weary of life as with a tale twice told.
Thou who dost know what ingrate subjects are,
Hear me, assoil, receive me, God, my God.

VIGIL.

JOY is dead, but Love doth sit,
    Faithful mourner, by his bed ;
Tender grass she cherisheth,
    Weedeth out the poppies red.
They may sleep whose dreams are sweet,
Love doth watch by quiet feet :
    Fall softly, rain, fall softly.

Joy was young, but Love so old,
    He grew weary over soon ;
She doth wait the evening light,
    He lay down and died at noon.
Quickly was Joy's sojourn past ;
Love was first and shall be last :
    Fall softly, rain, fall softly.

THE WOEFUL LADY.

THE snow it lay light, and the snow it lay cold,
  It carelessly covered the desolate wold.
As a lover that loves not doth smile on a maid,
So the moonlight and frost-light capriciously played;
And alone stood the woeful lady.

Her robe like a shadow did muffle her feet,
Her face from the camlet shone pitiful sweet;
Like a nun's was the dress, but her neck it was bare,
For a babe like a snow-flake lay shivering there;
And she wept, did the woeful lady.

" O my lover had sinned, had sinned,
So I left him and went my way;
And I clutched at Heaven, in robber guise;
It is Hell I have gained this day.

" Then he wedded my rival false,
And she bare him a babe so fair ;
But her soul grew dim, and its light went out,
And in madness she knew despair.

" And she slew him, my love, my love !
Rising up in the dead of night ;
And they say she wist not the thing she did,
But I know she had sore despite.

" And the babe it is mine, is mine,
But it never will thrive with me ;
For I loved the father, and spurned the mother,
And the two are gone home, Woe is me !"

The babe it awoke, and smiled up in her face,—
" Oh Jesu, Lord Jesu, grant succour, I pray !
Give us only a shelter until it be day."—
But the babe, it was weary, and sighed life away :
Oh, alas, for the woeful Lady !

"THERE THEY BURIED HIM."

OUT among the mountains
　　Where the breezes blow,
Where the little blue-bells
　　Wave to and fro;
There I went to bury
　　One old self of mine,
Covered it with mole-earth
　　Light and fine,
And beside it planted
　　A wild grape vine.

Out among the mountains
　　Again went I,
Windy rain was flashing
　　Across the sky ;
I was sorely weary,

And I cried in pain,
"Oh, my self I buried
Come to life again !"
Answered to my weeping
Only falling rain.

Out among the mountains
Came I once more ;
Summer sun was shining,
The storms were o'er ;
And a hand that loved me
Gathered of my vine
Tender grapes to cheer me,
Nectar passing wine ;
And two lips that loved me
Sealéd mine,
And a heart that loved me
Healéd mine.

BROKEN CHORDS.

BROKEN CHORDS.

L IKE the harmonies that struggle
　　Through the fugueing of an air ;
Thus I heard them, broken fragments,
　　From a music sweet and rare.

What the whole might be I know not ;
　　'Tis but mine to tell the tale
As I heard it, softly falling,
　　Through the twilight clear and pale.

HORTUS SICCUS.

ONE has some friendships, folded, put away,
    Pressed into memory's leaves, like withered
      flow'rs,
Which, though we know their bloom hath all departed,
We give more love to than we often say,
And still rejoice that we have called them ours,
And feel, because of them, the stronger-hearted.

And though we know one puff of healthy wind
Would soon reduce them to the dust they are,
One careless touch destroy their deadened beauty,
We only grow, because of that, more kind,
Avert more tenderly each threatened jar,
And count their cherishing a precious duty.

And when at eventide we are alone,
We bring them out, and live with them again,
And bygone fragrance seems to come upon them ;
The years all pass away which since have flown ;
A strange dull aching at the heart, like pain,
Reminds us how the sunbeams once fell on them.

PATIENCE.

YES, I will hush my heart, as though it were
    A weakling babe, that could be rocked to sleep
With gentle words and promises of good ;
    Dost hear, my little heart ? thou must not weep.

We will go softly through this tangled wood,
    Lest we, perchance, on some poor worm may tread,
Or brush against some panting wounded bird,
    And leave, what might have been the living, dead.

And, lest some fellow-traveller be lost,
    And spending in the darkness fruitless toil,
We will hold out a steady shining lamp,
    Although it burn our only cruse of oil.

Dost hear, my heart?   Ah no, thou must not moan,
　　We have not nearly learned our lesson yet ;
"Suppose the cruse should fail, and we should
　　　starve ? "
　　Let it be so, there is no need to fret.

'Tis only that the end of life is death,
　　And after death, we know, comes life again,
And immortality.—Dost say, poor heart,
　　That future bliss enhances present pain ?

Well, hush thee, for a moment, while I send
　　Across the darkness just one bitter cry :
" If there be any pilgrims farther on,
　　Turn back, I pray, and help us, or we die."

There comes no answer, deeper darkness falls,
　　And yet I am the better for my cry.
And thou, O perished heart ! O baby heart !
　　Within mine aching arms stone-dead dost lie !

Pure heart, good heart, we safely praise the dead ;
　　It died so young, and died so suddenly ;
And life is now so empty, and so still.—
　　Poor tender heart, the robins bury thee.

AGAINST TEARS.

THIS world is all too sad for tears,
   I would not weep, not I,
But smile along my life's short road,
   Until I, smiling, die.

The little flowers breathe sweetness out
   Through all the dewy night ;
Should I more churlish be than they,
   And 'plain for constant light ?

Not so, not so, no load of woe
   Need bring despairing frown ;
For while we bear it, we can bear,
   Past that, we lay it down.

CENSOR AND CAVILLER.

NETTLE-FLOWER and camomile
    Grew together, blooming,
Only for a little while ;
    Then the weed, presuming,
Thrust the wholesome herb aside,
And to all the garden cried,
" I succeed, where both have tried ; "
Then arose in vulgar pride,
    On its prowess pluming.

Camomile came slowly on,
    Half its strength concealing :
" Thou hast power to wound, alone ;
    Mine, though sharp, brings healing.
He that only smites to slay
Needs small skill, the hunters say ;
Gnat, that stings and flies away,
Needs still less, so all men say—
    Deeper truth revealing.

" He who feeds on nought but sweets
    Has but feeble being ;
He who knows but bitter meats
    Loses power of seeing.
'Tis our part to rectify,
Raise the low and brace the high."—
Thus the herb doth softly sigh.
All the breezes, passing by,
    Wave their wings, agreeing.

A LOST FRIEND.

DEAR, I dreamt of you last Sunday even ;
    Slumbrous was the sermon, and the heat
Weighed mine eyelids down, and summer perfumes
    Stole in on the breezes, slow and sweet :
Leaning back, I half thought—" God is tender,
    Will not chide my sleeping at His feet."

Swiftly, like the Mene and Upharsin,
    Came a name upon my vision thrown ;
Name of her who till one day, one moment,
    Was the noblest, rarest woman known.
Then the preacher's voice came through my slumbers,
    " He that sinneth not may cast a stone."

Oh, my darling ! drowned out past remembrance,
    Would that I had died for thee, my friend !
Any death that had but slain the body,
    Any death that with the life would end ;
If a message could but reach you, reach you,
    What beseeching prayer would I send !

In my dream she stood at rest beside me,
    As we used to stand so long ago,
Saying, "Little one, too much you love me."
    While I smiled, "Too much love cannot know."
Then there came the shadow o'er her features,
    Shade prophetic of the coming woe.

If I love her still does Christ not love her?
    I cannot forget, will He forget?
I have only will, who has the power
    Somehow—He knows how—will save her yet.
Dear lost jewel! till I find you, find you,
    I will wear my diamond in jet.

Thus I dreamed, then woke to hear the organ
    Pealing " Peace on earth, good-will to men,
Glory to the Father, Son, and Spirit,
    More than ever hath been shall be then;
When the 'angels have their great rejoicing,
    When the whole creation saith 'Amen.'"

LIGHT AT EVENING.

ALL these years!
And I have never known it, oh my God!
What had I done, that thou shouldst blind me so?
I feeling dumbly after other hearts
That cared not for me; this one all mine own.

Was it indeed so? didst thou draw me, dear,
By subtle spirit motion, that I knew
There was a soul that loved me in the world,
And knew not it was thine?

Fear me; how couldst thou? fear a butterfly,
A little beggar child upon the road,
A bird with broken wings, fear feeblest things,
But me, how couldst thou fear?

And now it is too late ; the very thing
That gives thee boldness takes my power away.
"Because I die, I tell thee," said thy lips ;
And mine can only close on them with tears.

How shall I serve thee ? how can I compress
The joy of our lost years into this space ?
Would thou couldst take me with thee on thy flight,
To follow thee, and serve as thou hast served.

Hast thou no wishes, nothing I ean do ?
One thing ?   Declare it.   That I keep my soul
Unspotted, train it for the highest things,
And hold myself as precious for thy sake ?
I promise it.

But for thyself, dear,—now that thou dost stand
With heaven in one hand, is there no gift
Thine other could receive ?   Command me, dear ;
I am all thine.

One thing ?   Thine epitaph upon my heart ?
It shall be graven there, burnt in and in :
Tell it me, I repeat it after thee,
"I truly might have loved him had I known."

So calm, so cold! Oh, God forgive me, dear!
I will go tenderly through all my days,
And when we meet out yonder, thou shalt know
I was not all unworthy, even of thee.

PETRARCA.

I KNEW a bard, Petrarca, who did sing
   His love-worn ditties, melancholy sweet,
And played upon his lute of single string
The dances suited to his weary feet,
Until 'twas said, " If this man had not loved, .
Had not been held so long in bitter thrall,
Then he a mighty hero-bard had proved,
Had soared above earth's sorrows mean and small."
But in the broken lute a spirit moved,—
" Had he not loved, he ne'er had sung at all."

LOOKING BACK.

LET him be God's, not mine,—'tis better so.
    I marred the music of his spirit's lute,
And brushed my hand too rudely through its strings :
        And now it lieth mute.

I might have gladdened him, and would not know,
And so there stepped an angel on the way,
And bore him past me, opening mine eyes.
        It is too late to-day.

I can but pray for him, ay, still will pray ;
Death is no farther off than life, I wis :
A deeper thrill of joy shall pulse through him,
        Ay, even 'mid Heaven's bliss.

MUSIC AT NIGHT.

RIPPLE of waves upon the moonlit shore,
 Chiming of voices silent evermore,
Shining of summer light on southern seas,
Murmur of doves among the forest trees,
 Perfume of growing vines and clover lea,
 Scent, sound, and sight they all come back to me—
All of delight my life hath ever known,
Gathered and scattered in one dulcet tone.

AGNUS DEI.

LAMB of God, whose awful beauty
  Shines within the darkest place,
So that devils veil their faces,
  And the little ones find grace:
    Agnus Dei, Agnus Dei!
  Suffer us Thy feet to trace.

Lamb of God, whose perfect whiteness
  Throws no shadow of a stain;
Suffer us Thy fallen spirits
  Something of Thy light to gain.
    Agnus Dei, Agnus Dei!
  Purify us by Thy pain.

Lamb of God, whose love so wondrous
On our callous natures came,
Making of our very passions
Fuel for Thy lambent flame.
Agnus Dei, Agnus Dei !
Sanctify us through Thy name,
Jesu Christe, Agnus Dei !
Amen.

LONDON: PRINTED BY W. CLOWES AND SONS, DUKE STREET, STAMFORD STREET,
AND CHARING CROSS.

Twilight Hours: a Legacy of Verse.

By SARAH WILLIAMS (Sadie).
Crown 8vo. 5*s.*

The Legends of King Arthur and his Knights of the Round Table.

Dedicated to Mr. Tennyson.
Small 8vo. Cloth, 1*s.* 6*d.*; paper cover, 1*s.*

How to Study the New Testament.

By HENRY ALFORD, D.D., Dean of Canterbury.
3 vols. Small 8vo. 3*s.* 6*d.* each.

Poems.

By M. B. SMEDLEY. Crown 8vo. 6*s.*

The Works of C. J. Vaughan, D.D., Vicar of Doncaster.

Popular Edition, in small 8vo. vols., 2*s.* 6*d.* each.

Book I. PLAIN WORDS ON CHRISTIAN LIVING.
[Others in the Press.

Child-World.

By the Authors of, and uniform with, "Poems written for a Child."
With Illustrations. Square 32mo. 3*s.* 6*d.*

Lives of Indian Officers.

Illustrative of the History of the Civil and Military Services of India. By JOHN WILLIAM KAYE. Popular Edition. 3 vols., crown 8vo. 6s. each.

"We say at once that more admirably-written and interesting narratives are scarcely to be found in any literature. Nobler subjects of biography could not have been chosen, and higher praise it is impossible to bestow on a writer than to say, as we do of this author, that he is fully equal to such a theme. . . . . Mr. Kaye's 'Lives of Indian Officers' will take a high place among the standard books of England."—*Athenæum.*

Eastward: Travels in Egypt, Palestine, and Syria.

By NORMAN MACLEOD, D.D. Popular Edition, with Illustrations. Crown 8vo. 6s.

"It is the most enjoyable book on the Holy Land we have ever read."—*Nonconformist.*

Practical Essays on Education.

By THOMAS MARKBY, M.A. Crown 8vo. 6s.

"Among the many essays that have been published on the subject Mr. Markby's are entitled to stand high both for their readableness and the judgment they display."—*London Review.* "Well worth reading."—*Spectator.*

The Disciple, and other Poems.

By GEORGE MACDONALD, LL.D., Author of "Within and Without," &c. Crown 8vo. 6s.

"Mr. MacDonald is, before all else, a poet. His poems are, after all, his best productions. . . . No extracts and no phrase of criticism could convey to the reader any idea of that peculiarly beautiful aroma of spirituality floating always in the moon-like tenderness of his manner, which constitutes the true individuality of Mr. MacDonald as a writer. Of its order this volume is unique, and it is full of wisdom, beauty, and exhilarating brightness."—*Illustrated Times.*

A Sister's Bye-hours.

By the Author of "Studies for Stories."
With Illustrations. Crown 8vo. 5*s.*

"We put this book down with regret. We have said enough to show that it is brimful of true, warm affection, and that it is as faultless in language as it is simple in style."—*London Review.*

On "Ecce Homo."

By the Right Hon. W. E. GLADSTONE.
Second Edition. Crown 8vo. 5*s.*

"A curiously delicate essay on the method pursued in 'Ecce Homo,' the fine and complicated texture of which is in strange contrast with the bold doubts and bold dogmatisms of modern thought."—*Spectator.*

The Reign of Law.

By the DUKE OF ARGYLL. Fifth and Cheaper Edition, with Additions. Crown 8vo. 6*s.*

"The aim of this book is lofty, and requires not only a thorough familiarity with metaphysical and scientific subjects, but a breadth of thought, a freedom from prejudice, a general versatility and sympathetic quality of mind, and a power of clear exposition rare in all ages and in all countries. We have no hesitation in expressing an opinion that all these qualifications are to be recognised in the Duke of Argyll, and that his book is as unanswerable as it is attractive."—*Pall Mall Gazette.*

Week-day Sermons.

By R. W. DALE, M.A.
Popular Edition. Crown 8vo. 3*s.* 6*d.*

"We can only recommend our readers to lay this volume of Mr. Dale's in stock as soon as·may be. For reading aloud, and exciting friendly discussion, we hardly know any modern book like it."—The Dean of Canterbury in the *Contemporary Review.*

"The freshness, the directness, the earnestness, and the practical good sense of these sermons must commend them to all thoughtful men."—*Nonconformist.*

Unspoken Sermons.

By GEORGE MACDONALD, LL.D.

Popular Edition. Crown 8vo. 3s. 6d.

"In George MacDonald's company the very air seems impregnated with love and purity and tenderness. We seem to be under an Italian sky. A loving heart reveals to us the heart which is the fountain of love, and sends us away ashamed of our harsh and bitter feelings, and praying to be able to love more both Him who is love and those who ought ever to be dear to us for His sake."—Dr. Guthrie's "*Sunday Magazine.*"

A French Country Family.

By MADAME DE WITT, *née* GUIZOT. Translated by the Author of "John Halifax, Gentleman." With Illustrations. Crown 8vo. 5s.

"Madame de Witt is a charming painter of the natures and ways of well-nurtured children, and the author of 'John Halifax, Gentleman,' has done good service in giving us this English version of a book which will delight the inmates of our nurseries."—*Athenæum.*

Scripture Portraits, and other Miscellanies.

From the Published Writings of A. P. STANLEY, D.D., Dean of Westminster. Crown 8vo. 6s.

"All these selections are conspicuous for the earnest and thoughtful grace peculiar to their author. It is superfluous to say more about extracts from books which have already achieved such high distinction, and which have brought both the characters and the scenery of the Bible home to English hearts and minds."—*Spectator.*

Days of Yore.

By SARAH TYTLER, Author of "Papers for Thoughtful Girls." Crown 8vo. 5s.

"The first tales in the volume give us some of the finest descriptions of scenery we have ever read, while the meditative mood into which Miss Tytler frequently falls in these eighteenth-century reminiscences is very like the delightful chit-chat with which Thackeray indulged his readers so often."—*Spectator.*

The Year of Praise.

Being Hymns, with Tunes, for the Sundays and Holidays of the Year.

Intended for use in Canterbury Cathedral, and adapted for Cathedral and Parish Churches generally.

Edited by HENRY ALFORD, D.D., Dean of Canterbury.

Assisted in the Musical Part by Robert Hake, M.A., Precentor, and Thomas Evance Jones, Organist, of Canterbury Cathedral.

*** This Book contains Four Hymns for every Sunday in the Year, the First Hymn in each case being adapted, as an Introit, to the special subject of the Sunday.

For public convenience, the YEAR of PRAISE is issued in four forms, namely :—

   I. LARGE TYPE, with MUSIC. Imperial 16mo., 3*s.* 6*d.*
  II. SMALL TYPE, with MUSIC. Crown 8vo., 1*s.* 6*d.*
 III. LARGE TYPE, without Music. Small 8vo., 1*s.*
 IV. SMALL TYPE, without MUSIC. Demy 18mo., 6*d.*

The Hymns of Denmark.

Rendered into English, by GILBERT TAIT.

Small 8vo., cloth extra. 4*s.* 6*d.*

Paul Gerhardt's Spiritual Songs.

Translated by JOHN KELLY. Small square 8vo. 5*s.*

Lights through a Lattice.

By J. E. A. BROWN. Small 8vo. 3*s.* 6*d.*

Annals of a Quiet Neighbourhood.

By George MacDonald, LL.D.

Popular Edition.   Crown 8vo.   6*s.*

" Whoever reads this story once will read it many times. It shows an almost supernatural insight into the workings of the human heart."—*Pall Mall Gazette.*

"This story is one that only a man of genius could have written." —*Examiner.*

The Christ of History.

By John Young, LL.D.

New and Enlarged Edition.   Crown 8vo.   5*s.*

" The republication of Dr. Young's ' Christ of History,' with an appendix on Renan's ' Vie de Jésus,' is well timed. The argument is irresistible and unanswerable. We trust that this reappearance of a work of such great excellence, eloquence, and logical compactness will give fresh impetus to its study, and lead those who persist in approaching Christ on the strictly human side to cry, with the Apostle, ' My Lord and my God.' "—*British Quarterly Review.*

The Romance of Charity.

Being an Account of some Remarkable Institutions on the Continent. By John de Liefde. With numerous Portraits and Illustrations. Crown 8vo.   5*s.*

"Mr. de Liefde may well call his volume 'The Romance of Charity,' for his collection of facts overpass fiction in strangeness. It is not very creditable that such vast works of Christian love should be absolutely unknown to, or unappreciated by, the approved leaders and principal advocates of our Church system in England. Some of the accounts given by Mr. de Liefde are most affecting and truly wonderful."—The Dean of Canterbury in the *Contemporary Review.*

Essays from " Good Words."

By Henry Rogers, Author of "The Eclipse of Faith." Small 8vo.   5*s.*

On the Written Word.

By the Rev. J. Oswald Dykes, M.A. Small 8vo.   2*s.* 6*d.*

Reminiscences of a Highland Parish.

By NORMAN MACLEOD, D.D. Popular Edition. Crown 8vo. 6s.

"One of the most refreshing and delightful books which can any-where be found. The impression which it makes is the nearest thing possible to the delight of wandering in fine autumn weather on the braesides of the mountains that look forth on the islands and the Atlantic. And the reader will find in the book what the mere wanderer cannot see in nature—a rich storehouse of noble humani-ties."—*Scotsman.*

Wind-wafted Seed.

Reprinted from "Good Words" and "The Sunday Magazine," edited by NORMAN MACLEOD, D.D., and THOMAS GUTHRIE, D.D. Crown 8vo. 3s. 6d.

Dr. Austin's Guests.

By WILLIAM GILBERT, Author of "Shirley Hall Asy-lum," &c. Popular Edition. Crown 8vo. 6s.

"This is one of the small number of works of current fiction that are not made only to be borrowed from a lending library, but are worth putting on one's book-shelves."—*Examiner.*

Studies of Character from the Old Testament.

By THOMAS GUTHRIE, D.D. Crown 8vo. 3s. 6d.

"Better reading for the family we have not ; and in an age like this, when, as heroes, we are tempted to worship men of rather small stature, it must be edifying, refreshing, and bracing to hold communion again with the giants of the patriarchal period. And here they are to be found in all their force, and fervour, and faith, not certainly 'without spot or blemish,' but in the light and shades alike of their virtues and their failings."—*Literary World.*

Poems.

By DORA GREENWELL. Enlarged Edit. Crown 8vo. 6s.

"Here is a poet as true as George Herbert or Henry Vaughan or our own Cowper. We advise our readers to possess the book, and get the joy and the surprise of so much real thought and feeling. It is a cardiphonia set to music."—*North British Review.*

La Belle France.

By BESSIE PARKES BELLOC, Author of "Vignettes," "Essays on Woman's Work," &c. Square 8vo. 12s.

"These sketches were all written on the spot which they describe, and the actual local colouring as well as that of tradition has been very naturally caught. There is not one line of the guide-book element, for all the descriptions are those of an artist. The revelling in architecture, and scenery, the pictures of peasant life, the stories of the present day, and of the years long past, cannot fail to be pleasing to the reader."—*Illustrated Times*.

Wealth and Welfare.

By JEREMIAH GOTTHELF.

Popular Edition. Crown 8vo. 6s.

"For a long time we have not read a book in which the style was at once so fresh and individual without being forced. The work is a perfect little mine of shrewd observation."—*London Review*.

London Poems.

By ROBERT BUCHANAN. Crown 8vo. 5s.

"We hardly know of any narrative poetry greater than is found in some of these sad and mourning lines. . . . These verses have been lived before they were written down."—*Athenæum*.

"No volume has appeared for many years in London which so certainly announces a poetic fame."—*Spectator*.

A Summer in Skye.

By ALEXANDER SMITH.

Popular Edition. Crown 8vo. 6s.

"There are passages in the present volume which show the author's marvellous power of reproducing at will the magnificent effects of mountain scenery—passages in which a play of fancy and a true poetic insight strongly reinforce an illustration already presented with great facility of expression and rich colouring."—*Nonconformist*.

The Tragedies of Sophocles.

Newly translated, with a Biographical Essay. By E. H. PLUMPTRE, M.A., Professor of Divinity, King's College, London. Popular Edition, with an Appendix of Rhymed Choruses. Crown 8vo. 7s. 6d.

"Let us say at once that Professor Plumptre has not only surpassed the previous translators of Sophocles, but has produced a work of singular merit, not less remarkable for its felicity than its fidelity ; a really readable and enjoyable version of the old plays." —*Pall Mall Gazette.*

Familiar Lectures on Scientific Subjects.

By Sir JOHN F. W. HERSCHEL, Bart.

Crown 8vo. 6s.

"A book of most profound and romantic scientific charm. . . Without any strain of manner, the author paints picture after picture from the wonderful discoveries made known to us by the study of the physical forces at work on the earth and in the heavens."—*Spectator.*

A Year at the Shore.

A Companion Book for the Sea-side. By PHILIP HENRY GOSSE, F.R.S. With Thirty-six Illustrations by the Author, printed in Colours. Crown 8vo. 6s.

"A delicious book deliciously illustrated."—*Illustrated London News.*

The Progress of the Working Class, 1832–67.

By J. M. LUDLOW and LLOYD JONES.

Small crown 8vo. 2s. 6d.

"We recommend every politician who values his reputation, and every intelligent working-man with half-a-crown to spare, to purchase and read it at his earliest opportunity."—*Spectator.*

Essays.

By DORA GREENWELL. Crown 8vo. 6s.

CONTENTS :—1. Our Single Women.—2. Hardened in Good.—3. Prayer.—4. Popular Religious Literature.—5. Christianos ad Leones.

" Miss Greenwell's Essays are very graceful, and are written with a real knowledge of their subjects. The book is really a good one."—*Spectator.*

"We highly value all the Essays for their good sense, fine feeling, and hearty religiousness, and for the freshness and piquancy of their style. Together they form one of the most admirable pleas for, and defences of, Christian philanthropy which have lately issued from the press."—*Nonconformist.*

Studies for Stories from Girls' Lives.

With Illustrations. Crown 8vo. 5s.

"Simple in style, warm with human affection, and written in faultless English, these five stories are studies for the artist, sermons for the thoughtful, and a rare source of delight for all who can find pleasure in really good works of prose fiction. . . . . They are prose poems."—*Athenæum.*

The Diamond Rose: a Life of Love and Duty.

By SARAH TYTLER, Author of "Papers for Thoughtful Girls," &c. Crown 8vo. 5s.

"Story sweetly told. It is so full of character, it has such a depth of true human pathos about it, and—what in these days is no small merit—it is written in such an exquisitely perfect style, that we hope all our readers will procure it for themselves."—*Literary Churchman.*

Views and Opinions.

By MATTHEW BROWNE. Crown 8vo. 6s.

"Mr. Matthew Browne's volume of essays is the work of a highly sensitive and cultivated mind. There is a rare and original vein of sportive humour running throughout its pages. . . . These are rare qualities ; and the book in which they are displayed has few if any recent equals."—*Westminster Review.*

Stories Told to a Child.

With Illustrations. Square 32mo. 3s. 6d.

"There is more real faculty in some of these brief tales than could be found by analysis in half the successful novels now published. One most pleasant thing about the book is, that though it is written for children by a brain capable of instructing the minds and ennobling the thoughts of grown people, there is no *coming down* to nursery intellects. The author's efforts are simply wide enough to embrace them, and Catholic enough to be to them like the wholesome sunshine and wind. More than this it is not easy to say, but that may be said with entire confidence."—*Pall Mall Gazette.*

Dealings with the Fairies.

By GEORGE MACDONALD, LL.D. With Illustrations by Arthur Hughes. Square 32mo. 2s. 6d.

"The growth of imaginativeness, a great desideratum in our young people, will not be to be despaired of if their fancy is but nursed on such a pleasant blending of allegory and reality as Mr. MacDonald purveys in the 'Golden Key' and his other 'Dealings with the Fairies.'"—*Saturday Review.*

Poems Written for a Child.

By TWO FRIENDS.
With Illustrations. Square 32mo. 3s. 6d.

"In these poems there is a delicacy and vividness of description, a humorous grace and perfect knowledge of childhood, which give them a very high rank, not only as children's poems, but as poems about childhood. . . . Wordsworth might have envied these happy cadences, these tender touches of impersonation."—*Pall Mall Gazette.*

Lilliput Levee: Poems of Childhood, Child-fancy, and Childlike Moods.

With Illustrations. Square 32mo. 2s. 6d.

"This author will be established as the children's poet for, at all events, this present generation. . . . Read it all you lucky young folks, and be grateful to your benefactor the unknown writer of 'Lilliput Levee.'"—*Chambers's Journal.*